LIGHT SHIFTS

Light Shifts
First published: December 2021
Printed in the United States of America
ISBN: 978-1-7359752-3-8

ALL RIGHTS RESERVED. Except as permitted under the U.S. Copyright Act of 1976, no part of this publication may be reproduced, distributed, or transmitted in any form or by any means, or stored in a database or retrieval system, without the prior written permission of Carole Di Tosti.

This book was published by A Priori Publishing.

Copyright © 2021 by Carole M. Di Tosti

LIGHT SHIFTS

‡

Carole Di Tosti

Author of the blog *A Christian Apologist's Sonnets*

For Leyna

CONTENTS

ACKNOWLEDGEMENTS

Prologue: **Poets**

SHADES OF DARK AND LIGHT

Vanquished	1
On Writing	2
The Dark Joker	3
On Seeing Nicholas Nickleby on Broadway	4
Dynamic Relationships	6
Remembering Your Love	7
Waxing Love	8
Artist's Purpose	9
Transformed to Agape Love	10
Spiritual, Earthly Love	11
Heavenly Validation	12
Elusive Truth	14
A Vision	15
Fall From Grace	16
Clarity	17

IN MEMORIAM

In Memoriam	21
Anthony Bourdain	22
Carrie Fisher	24
Philip Seymour Hoffman	26
Whitney Houston	28
Mike Nichols	30
Peter O'Toole	32
Gore Vidal	34
Toni Morrison	36
Leyna Gabriele	38
Cicely Tyson	40
Terrance McNally	42
Requiem For Edgar Allan Poe	44

POLITICS AND RELIGION

A Prayer for National Reconciliation	49
The Golden Calf and Mammon	50

Christ's Law of Love: A Woman's Right to Choose	52
Galileo Galilei and God	54
To Unify the Nation	55
Black Lives Matter	56
The Spirit of Hypocrisy	58
Justice, Rights, Freedom: In the Name of God!	60
C.S. Lewis and Agape Love	62
When Minds Are Closed	64
United States of America	65
Political Arrogance	66
Trolls	67
A Politician's Hard Redemption	68
Redeem Our Betrayal of Our Nation	69
The Church Seduction	70
Revocation of the Unapologetic	71
Trade Market	72
Requited Love is Christmas	73
Resurrection After COVID-19	74

SONNETS OF THE SOUL

Soul Trials	79
The Lost Psychiatrist	80
Soul Struggle	82
Shattering	84
Floating	85
My Love of God Grows Deeper Every Day	86
Surcease	87
I Feel My Christian Soul	88
Shaking Off Despair	89
I Wake to Face The Night	90
Last Night a Spectral Figure	91
The Hands of Guilt	92
To Trust Oneself, a Paradox	93
I Call Upon The Lord	94
Why Do I Fear?	95
While Steeped in Nervous Thoughts	96
I've Gone From Hope and Life	97
Such Darkness and Depression	98
Move	99
The Prophet Israel	100
A New Creation	101
Savior	102
The Lord	103
Incomplete	104
The Soul of Alzheimer's	105

Breaking Through	108
Blind	110
The Dark Will Never Understand the Light	111

GOD IN NATURE

Lotus	115
Red-tailed Hawks and Mourning Doves	116
Cat Human	117
Galaxies	118
Sanctuary	119
Orchidaceae	120
Sparrows	122
Fifty Shades of Fall	124
The Last Lotus	125

The truth is rarely pure and never simple.

                                                             -OSCAR WILDE

Do not go where the path may lead. Go instead where there is no path and leave a trail.

                                            -RALPH WALDO EMERSON

It is during our darkest moments that we must focus to see the light.

                                                             -ARISTOTLE

There is neither Jew nor Gentile, neither slave nor free, nor is there male and female, for you are all one in Christ Jesus.

                        BIBLE, NEW INTERNATIONAL VERSION, GALATIANS 3:28

ACKNOWLEDGEMENTS

Light Shifts would not have happened but for Fred Feirstein. I met Fred in a *Theatre Resources Unlimited* producer's workshop. With another member, we were responsible for a project. All three of us shared emails to schedule our work sessions. I had a cursory knowledge of my teammates but got to know them better when we met to discuss the project.

Before our first team meeting, Fred and I communicated via emails. Fred mentioned that he had read my blog *A Christian Apologist's Sonnets*. In the closing of my email, the poetry blog link is listed with the links of the other magazine outlets I write for. I am wont to be dismissive about my writing, always anxious to move on to another assignment, another poem, a theater review, play, etc. Thus, I assume most who answer my emails don't go below my closing to note the listed links. However, Fred did. He commented that he really enjoyed my sonnets. I was dense and didn't pick up the clues that only a poet and writer would be interested in another's poetry.

Our team met a few times and we got to know each other and agreed about how the musical project should be approached. At those meetings, while we waited for everyone to show up, Fred praised my poetry and said he thought it should be published in a book of poems. I was dismissive. He recognized that I did not take him at his word and affirmed twice, "Carole, I'm serious about this." I demurred that I found it difficult to take praise. He said he wanted to put me in touch with his publisher because my sonnets were important. They helped him and resonated with him. He felt an imperative to tell me because the sonnets could help others.

The last time I saw Fred before I flew to the UK in December 2019 with friends, he handed me a copy of his poetry book *Dark Energy* which I will treasure always. Because we became involved with the discussion of how to approach the musical play with our producer mentor, I was distracted and didn't ask Fred to sign my copy of *Dark Energy*. Not to worry, I thought. I knew that I would be working with Fred and my other teammate after I flew back from the UK.

That never came to be. When I returned, I emailed Fred a number of times. He didn't respond. I was worried. Then, his son, David, contacted me. Fred had passed away. The family were in mourning and trying to get through the days. I was devastated and expressed my condolences to David and told him his father was a special person that I was glad to have known for the brief period we collaborated.

I had read Fred's trenchant poetry in *Dark Energy*. He's a powerful poet. The poems are marked by lovely imagery, rhythm and rhyme schemes. The themes are profligate with wisdom. As I read, I was unable to forgive myself that I didn't have Fred sign my copy when he gave his book to me. Fate and final destinations have a way of creeping up and we don't realize it until…

At some point after all this, I looked up Frederick Feirstein online. I nearly collapsed. He had an amazing track record: he was a playwright with New York productions under his belt. He wrote screenplays and was a TV writer. Most importantly, he was a prize-winning poet of renown. I was devastated all the more about his comments to me on our last meeting. That meeting has haunted me, and I have felt compelled to put my sonnets in a book of poetry as an acknowledgement to Fred's artistic, poetic, generous soul. This is what I found in one of the poetry bios about him.

> **Frederick Feirstein** is a playwright with a dozen New York productions. He also writes for film and television and has had eight books of poetry published, two of which were nominated for the Pulitzer Prize. Among his literary awards are a Guggenheim Fellowship in Poetry, the Poetry Society of America's John Masefield Award, England's Arvon Prize for Poetry, and the Rockefeller Foundation's OADR Award for Playwriting. He was co-founder of the Expansive Poetry

movement and originated the Barnes & Noble reading series. His latest book of poems is *Dark Energy*.

Dark Energy is a spellbinding event, a major new book from one of our living masters of formal (that is, musical) poetry. The immense sequence "Gravity of the Black Hole" weaves fairy tale, classic myth, and modern psychology into a seamless tapestry, abounding in ironies and keen insights into the lives we lead. Moreover, a generous rasher of strong new Feirstein poems completes one of the standout collections of this or any year. — X. J. Kennedy

Dark Energy is a feast served up by a master poet. In the opening sequence, Feirstein had a few helpers—in the kitchen, Dr. Freud, the Brothers Grimm, Walt Disney—their insights and characters. In the anteroom, the ghosts of Mozart, Dickinson, and William Blake. Prowling the outer dark, death in its myriad forms, and masks. In the second sequence, Feirstein, the poet of dream, myth and fantasy becomes the narrative, mortal, poet of modern Manhattan and its own myths. Manhattan's myths slowly lose their glitter. The dark prowler steps out from the shadows. The poetry is triumphant. — Clark Blaise

This savvy, savage, and moving book of poems from Frederick Feirstein, a Master formalist at the height of his powers, takes as its motto "Teach us to be courageous and naïve." Feirstein knows the human condition as only a seen-it-all psychotherapist can, and he uses his adroit rhymes to make his insights sing in *Dark Energy*, a series of gimlet-eyed and sometimes laugh-out-loud funny riffs on the material of fairy tales. From the witch's oven in Hansel and Gretl to the ovens of concentration camps, from Red Riding Hood to Freud, *Dark Energy* is replete with memorable aphorisms that make the transient nature of the world comprehensible. In these lucid, direct, thoroughly unsentimental poems from a wise man who is also a romantic, Feirstein offers a rich appreciation of what it means to be alive. — Molly Peacock

If you are a poet and even if you believe you aren't, his website, frederickfeirstein.com, has valuable articles about poetry that might interest you.

Light Shifts has been published following Fred's adjuration. And it is my sincerest hope that these sonnets impact, soothe, help and in some way touch all who read them. Yes, Fred, I do take you seriously.

Carole Di Tosti, August, 2021

Prologue

POETS

Throughout the ages poets stand time still,

Refine the infinite so it can be gleaned,

Renew the inner life to make fulfilled

The spiritual self in glory great, redeemed.

With rhyming verse, with images clear, opaque,

With sensate rhythms felt in beats they sound,

These poets stir, and thrill, and strike, and wake

Us to ourselves, impact our souls. Profound!

Sometimes all consciousness does thrum with Grace,

And other times the darkness, pain and woe

Occlude the light, propel us toward stark fate

Where conflicts smite with searing, raging blows.

Tis then we seek the poets' prescient gaze,

Uplift our hearts and brighten sorrowful days.

SHADES OF DARK AND LIGHT

✥

VANQUISHED

Oh X*! I do proclaim your plans are naught.

The system that you worship is destroyed.

The idols you have built and daily sought

Are empty, death-filled, cannot be deployed.

The beauty you embrace disintegrates,

For underneath it's filled with dead men's bones.

Your golden dream is not a solid state.

It dissipates. You face its void alone.

Oh! See the Light bestows Truth to your soul.

No lies can hide within its loving grace.

It draws you to its warmth. Dispels the cold,

Of hatred's isolation and disgrace.

Forever let these words of wisdom guide

You toward Christ's Truth, so Spiritually you abide.

*X stands for whomever you proclaim

ON WRITING

I wrote this sonnet in Professor Margo Ely's Ethnography class, a requirement for my Ph.D. at New York University in the School of Education. It was in her class that I became confident of all genres of writing and employed them in the ethnography narratives of my dissertation which is published. I am forever grateful to her maverick soul, gumption, and grace. With determination she launched out where other professors refused to go. (1993)

The time is NOW to summon all my strengths,
Discerning vision, wisdom, the writer's arts,
And untie fetters that would halt the length,
The breadth, the height, the width of a writer's heart.
Immerse myself in Truth's quixotic way,
And force no labeled notions preconceived,
Be ready for imagination's day,
And place my hope in serendipity.
To story tell, I write in paradox.
I ebb and flow the joy, my soul dismay,
And mine the spiritual gold, defy time's shocks,
Withstand enthusiasms and delays.
Surprise! The treasures seen…discoveries won,
Expressed, redeeming love of God's Dear Son.

THE DARK JOKER

He's here again, the Joker of Dark Thoughts.

He beckons me to swim in his despair,

Inducing me to drink his poisoned draughts

And bludgeon bloody my soul beyond repair.

He strikes my heart with negativities,

Impales my mind with envy, loss, and pain,

Aligns me with the lazy and diseased,

Fires my mania HOT, gaslights my brain.

Look here! This artist's work eclipses yours.

And there! That one's success climbs to the stars.

And lo, you groundling, crawling on all fours,

Hang back to journey nowhere, near nor far.

Oh! Exorcise the joker while you can.

Confront his lies with Truth. In Christ then stand.

ON SEEING NICHOLAS NICKLEBY ON BROADWAY

The Royal Shakespeare Company's 1980 production of The Life and Adventures of Nicholas Nickleby was originally presented in London, UK at the Aldwych Theatre over two evenings, or in its entirety from early afternoon with a dinner break. Later, it was presented on television over four evenings. The production transferred to Broadway in the fall of 1981. I saw it in previews. I was gobsmacked and could not stop talking about it to my friends. I had never seen such alive, authentic performances. I sensed the greatness of the work. Roger Rees was the lead, Nicholas Nickleby, David Threlfall played Smike and Ben Kingsley was Squeers. After I saw it, I was never the same again. My veneration for theater had grown heaps. I knew I had witnessed something extraordinary but could only write a poem.

The play was adapted by David Edgar from the Charles Dickens novel The Life and Adventures of Nicholas Nickleby. It was directed by John Caird and Trevor Nunn. The music and lyrics were from Stephen Oliver and the set design was by John Napier and Dermot Hayes. It transferred to the Plymouth Theatre on Broadway, initially opening 4 October 1981, running until 3 January 1982. (1981)

ON SEEING NICHOLAS NICKLEBY ON BROADWAY

I saw perfection holy and complete

On Plymouth stage tonight, a heavenly space.

The actors' truthfulness magnificent feat,

As they inhabited characters with loving Grace.

The theme, redemption poignant and profound,

Did touch our hearts and shake us to the core.

The actors so alive they did astound.

Such wellsprings flowed from God, an open door.

The play uplifts the One who mercy brings,

The recompense of Smike, outcast and lost.

It shows the love of Christ toward human beings,

And those rejecting Christ at sorrowful cost.

My spirit was exalted by this play.

In love for artists who show us Truth's way.

DYNAMIC RELATIONSHIPS

Viewing the power struggle between individuals in the play The Caretaker (BAM Harvey Theater 2012) was revelatory. Egos were the problem, humanity the potential cure; the inability to touch another's soul, the devastation. How does one connect? Through compassion, through empathy, through the Spirit. But before that is possible, one must be in the Spirit and to do that is impossible if one is flesh, ego, pride. Only with God is such compassion and empathy possible. Harold Pinter who wrote the play revealed the emptiness and loneliness of humanity in crystal clear dialogue that the wonderful Spirit and humanity of the actors brought to life in the production. There was no perceived answer for humanity's abyss, no cure. Faith can bring the cure, but it is impossible without the electricity of Spirit to convey Hope. A beginning might be Psalm 23rd and prayer.

When egos step between our soul and mind,
When consciousness does sleep, is unaware
That we manipulate our past unkind
To get through tribulations so unfair.
When others drag us through their cruelties
And make us bow to their warped childhood blights
And wipe their dross on us like we're debris
And trash to dump in pits to fire their sight.
Then call upon the Lord and pray for strength
And vision to untangle any web
That's bound you up. Spiritually, you can rent
The chains, that do enslave your soul and ebb
The Grace. So, seek The Joy, The peace, The Light.
Destroy all bindings with Christ's loving Might.

REMEMBERING YOUR LOVE

I've had no time to conjure up your face

Or ponder your strange words to me that night.

Somehow, I've barely kept a steady pace

With tasks and work and problems that seem trite.

I've longed to catch my breath and write some lines

In memory of the vision that is you.

But chained I am to form and space and time,

That throttle all my soul in dark, bleak hues.

But now somehow your face comes to the fore,

Though other obstacles stand in the way.

And I can't blind my mind nor stop my core,

From dwelling on your being every day.

Until my spirit links with yours somehow,

Suppressed, am I entangled in Life's Now.

WAXING LOVE

As I reach out in comfort and self-love,

I feel you grow disconsolate and tense.

As I gain strength and cheerfully do strive,

My intuition feels your soul grow dense.

Oh, paradox that I should be the one

To elevate the baser part of you.

When I did seek a man, who'd say he's done,

With cursory ways and condemnations' hues.

As I seek Christ to gain relief in Life,

I watch you shelter in a love purloined.

As I touch you and offer more than wife,

You show your need for safety, with me join.

Establish trust! So, love the me in you.

Uplift your soul to find God loves you, too.

ARTIST'S PURPOSE

My purpose is revealed in time and space.

Acuity assures my seasoned view.

All doubts and woes and fears, I did erase,

When critics' condemnations I eschewed.

All time and fate are brothers under Christ,

Who works the plans and tunes our instruments,

Then moves sweet, sacred fingers to entice,

The artistry from our souls in recompense.

All artists do reflect eternity,

As vessels of a higher spirit must.

Compelled they are to aid posterity,

And prove that we aren't quintessential dust.

Artistic purpose dwells, compelled by Christ,

Bonds us with Grace the artist's sacrifice.

TRANSFORMED TO AGAPE* LOVE

I'm snared by your dark sensuality,

A caged hummingbird who's nectar crazed.

Your photograph rings sensual memories

Of secret passionate times, of weeks and days.

We've shared our bountiful beings living force,

Electrified our souls and fed desire.

Unified of spirit we set our course,

And soared above earth's selfish, angry fires.

Convinced, we travel on impassioned lines.

Mistaken we slip up, tread leaden space,

And free fall twisting to the edge of time.

But Christ does catch us with his hope and Grace.

We are conjoined. In spiritual love we grow,

In God whose gifts on us he has bestowed.

*Agape love is an unjealous, spiritual love bringing forgiveness and strength to let another be free

SPIRITUAL, EARTHLY LOVE

Time's specter is arrested when I gaze,

Upon the curve your form etches in space.

And sluttish passage of the years and days,

Cesate when vision I your sensual face.

The Kingdoms of the World are shadowed dust,

Fleshly heaps strewn round by Death's scythed hands.

The memory of your love is firmer crust,

On which to consummate God's fertile plans.

As primal selves we couple and conjoin,

Our spirits which fuse Love's eternal flame.

Then world and dust and time are thus purloined,

As we blaze forth the glory of Christ's name.

Together we embrace the universe,

In Christ and overcome self-hatred's curse.

HEAVENLY VALIDATION

I read Proof of Heaven, Dr. Eben Alexander's book about his N.D.E. (near death experience). Usually words come easily to me, but I find it difficult to describe the book's impact, except to say that its truths resonated and its life affirmations elucidating realms in the afterlife comforted me. It was a confirmation of my faith in God, the Spiritual realms of reality, Christ's unconditional love. If that does not work for you, then imagine feelings of intense relief and safety, warmth, love, joy and the sense that everything you thought might be good and true and positive, actually is.

Another way to relate it to you is imagine that someone of great authority and wisdom comes to you, and with sincerity, tells you that everything is OK and all is well. They insist that you shouldn't fear anything because ultimately, you are loved, and you should love yourself. They also affirm that there are beautiful unseen forces around you which are holding you up and shepherding you to the next level in your growth spiral. Just because science cannot adequately explain what happens to consciousness, the soul/life cycle, does not mean you, your being will end just because in materialism, physical bodies grow cold. There is much more to being and it is more incredible than you can possibly imagine.

You already know this. In fact, there have been glimpses of this eternity of infinite spirit throughout your entire life. If you stop to think about the strange coincidences, the weird happenings, the dreams, or intuitions that came true, you will remember. There is something tugging at you. It is drawing you and letting you know...there's more to reality than what your 5 senses apprehend...there is much more and it's great.

So when I had the opportunity to take the workshop with Dr. Eben Alexander and Karen Newel of Sacred Acoustics (there are frequencies of sound that can facilitate your stepping past the veil of materialism) at Omega Institute in upstate NY, I jumped at the chance. This sonnet inspired by their work is something I started in the class and finished when I returned home to NYC.

HEAVENLY VALIDATION

The pulsing flames of Light within soul life

Are solid waves of love, health and well-being.

Consciousness sublime of pure insight,

Transforms to unconditional love and spirit seeing.

The material world and all that it imbues,

Its social trends, its values we obey,

Our belief in science, empiricism's views,

Occludes our inner sight, our soul, betrays.

The powerful spiritual realms can't be obtained

Through fleshly sight and fleshly ego's pride:

Material things pervert our thoughts and stain

The truth by misdirection's stolid lies.

Eternity is real, can be embraced,

Within our consciousness through love and grace.

ELUSIVE TRUTH

Elusive truth's a phantom in this world.

Where topsy turvy values march their ways,

And wickedness spins cultural lies in whirls,

And harms our souls and makes ourselves betray.

Our inner truth transcends raw, ragged time.

It upholds spiritual love, self-confidence.

It manifests life's hope in pure sweet rhymes,

Brings harmony to logic and good sense.

Christ knew the world's "reality" was lies.

Was sacrificed by blind, ignoble men,

Who murdered truth and fostered evil ties

To Lucifer, deceiving us again.

Christ's life is truth for all of us to see.

Our faith in Christ is truth's reality.

A VISION

A vision! I did see the flames of Life

Thrust skyward, radiant, orange, yellowed hues,

Striated mixtured palettes dare not strike,

Unless the brush Divine, the paint of Truth.

And streaming up into horizon's dread,

A cold, coal-black, cruel silhouetted form

Did pierce the atmosphere upraised its head,

Threw down the fiery Light of Love's strong arms.

The Horse of Death* does come to buy and sell

Our souls for riches, bitcoin, property,

Parades his Kingdom's lures his graves to swell,

And mock the Cross, the Bread, the Wine, and thee.

But lo it's outward show, pretense that's fake.

Revealed Christ's Truth. We keep the first estate.

---

a figurative symbol of one of the four horsemen of the Apocalypse, Death, a spiritual collapse

FALL FROM GRACE

My neighbor! Don't despair a fall from grace!

For Christ's forgiveness cleanses all our acts.

The blindness that led you to soul's disgrace,

Corrected by the Word, redemption's fact.

And those corrupt who did encourage you,

Condemned they are to suicide themselves.

Together you succumbed to evil's truth,

So drawn by Mammon's lures not Godly wealth.

We are ordained to hear the Word of Life

And come to greater knowledge of The Grace,

Dispel our ego's pride that creates strife,

And follow in The Love to run Faith's race.

Count greatest as Christ's love and greatest wrought,

Christ's wisdom, thus, receive God's Divine Thought.

CLARITY

Before Foundation's crystals spoke the Truth,

Before Foundation's matrix formed starbursts,

Before Foundations' gemstones shattered loose,

Before we fell in knowledge, Adam's curse,

I saw with infinite vision God's design.

I heard the silence of that mighty work.

I touched the Life the Holy Fire refined.

I smelled the fragrance of the glorious Word.

Then I received. And then my soul felt Peace.

I knew the Earth was cradled in God's care.

Regardless of the darkness and Hell's lease,

My soul was Light, free from Hell's dark despair.

Christ's chosen and elect we do stay free,

In Light-filled peace and Faith, God's Glory see.

IN MEMORIAM

☦

IN MEMORIAM

We celebrate dear lives when they do pass,

Sweet souls who graced us when upon this earth,

Remind we mortals nothing ever lasts.

So, check ourselves and question our soul worth.

We're living on this plane of consciousness

A vast and hallowed sea of vibrant life.

How do we measure? What lives have we blessed?

Who did we help gain peace and calm their strife?

Death comes for all. So hard to face that truth.

The breath and blood that pumps will stop, cessate!

And Death's the terror of all naïve youth

But never feared when life's lived to create.

So, celebrate yourself from day to day.

Say in memoriam to self-hate's soul decay.

ANTHONY BOURDAIN

I had the opportunity to see Anthony Bourdain speak a number of times live: once at SXSW (South By Southwest, a festival in Austin, Texas) another time at The Barkley Center. He was always entertaining, raw and powerful. At the Barkley Center I sat behind his second wife and Eric Ripert, the Michelin Star Le Bernardin owner and his close friend who was staying in the same hotel in France when Anthony Bourdain took his life.

I also had the opportunity to interview him briefly at Tribeca Film Festival about two films he was in and helped produce with Lydia Tenaglia's Zero Point Zero Productions. They are excellent must see documentaries: Wasted! The Story of Food Waste (2017) and Jeremiah Tower: The Last Magnificent (2016). My brief interviews with him are on my YouTube channel.

His suicide was a shock. My friends and I mourned because he had so much to live for and had come so far. I guess he felt that the emotional pain was insupportable to get to the next day. I will always doubt his suicide. It is more upsetting for me to think he ended his life by his own hand, than if someone had put a hit out on him. In the last analysis, the latter rationale is farfetched and moves to conspiracies and QAnon, so I suffer, thinking this beautiful soul said, "I've had enough. I'm done, here."

ANTHONY BOURDAIN

Sage, cajoling humor trailed your life,

Beloved by friends and family and your fans,

Who spanned all ages, genders, races, types,

By you enthralled: the soulful, traveling man.

It's not that you impressed us with the sights,

Or sumptuous foods described with clarity.

Oh no! It was your expansive, deep insights,

Perfuming the air with your humanity.

Breaking bread with strangers, no regrets,

You shared your winsome grace with all you saw.

So struck by you, the show's guests would effect

Connections timeless which left us in awe.

You chose to leave all those who loved you so.

Forever remembered! On you our love bestowed.

CARRIE FISHER

I saw Carrie Fisher on Broadway in Wishful Drinking and was impressed by her mental acuity and self-effacing humor. It is no small feat to look squarely at one's painful weaknesses, and with searing irony, cauterize bleeding soul wounds, then publicly feed oneself and others from the kernels of wisdom produced by the process.

Nightly on Broadway and in her shows in LA, with light-saber humor, she slashed regrets and self-victimization with truth and grace. I, and those around me, with smiles on our faces, healed. She punctured our every "Hollywoodland" balloon fantasy and the ridiculous notions we harbored about Princess Leia and being a film icon. She offered herself up with a wide-armed embrace as our mentor proclaiming, "Yes, we have all experienced the shit storm, and we can weather it without swallowing too much crap or dying of E. coli poisoning."

Carrie, you moved from being the Star Wars' two-dimensional princess to an infinitely dimensional Queen. I imagine your consciousness in free flight soaring and communing in health and wholeness, thrilled that one element of your purpose on this planet has been fulfilled. R.I.P. We are the finer for having had your presence with us for a short time.

CARRIE FISHER

You sliced your pride with swords of truth and light

With honesty and grace so singular,

With soulful generosity to spite

Your perfect image; T'was overthrown! You stirred

Us to accept ourselves, love and forgive,

Because there's health if faults you learn to share

With others, so you're not afraid to live,

And turn from ego darkness and despair.

The process moved you to a grander place

Within our hearts, and we did empathize,

With all that you encountered and did face.

Truth burned the roots of all that you despised.

Remembered always Carrie you will be,

Your strength, your joy, your soul's dear majesty.

PHILIP SEYMOUR HOFFMAN

One of the great actors of our time, Philip Seymour Hoffman battled addiction. That knowledge and empathy of what OCD disorders do to one's being helped solidify the human reality behind the characters he portrayed. Days before 9/11 I saw him at a NYC airport. One of the first to deplane, he trundled out of the jetway. To others he was unrecognizable. Though he was his same disheveled self, hair electrified, clothes crumpled as if he had slept in them for days, he was intentionally blending. Talented actors are chameleons, masking their identity, hungrily anticipating a new character to "wear" like a fine tuxedo or gown.

I recognized the shy, invisible and called him by name, saying, "I love ya, man." When I proclaimed he would win an Oscar one day, his face flushed in high embarrassment. But then, he tossed over his shoulder wryly, "Thank you," and scurried like a crab back into anonymity. Of course, he did win for Capote (2005) five years later. That didn't help to thwart "the enemy" that he managed to conquer for a time. Then, one day it reared its ugly head and devoured him. Speechless with pain at his loss, Broadway acknowledged him, and Mark Rylance performing in Twelfth Night held a brief moment of silence during intermission. Mike Nichols, Hoffman's director of Arthur Miller's Death of a Salesman was in the audience.

PHILIP SEYMOUR HOFFMAN

You traveled to the depths of our despair,

And mined the gold of human tragedy.

Cloaked your being with our traits, prepared

Such complex characters, in empathy.

Unique, unparalleled and fearless too,

You searched your soul for evil and disgrace,

Immersed, inhabited that hellish truth,

Translated it; in you we saw our face.

Through you we saw, we're all the same within.

Black hearts, dark holes of boundless emptiness.

Unrequited vacuum, self-hate's "sin,"

The endless pain, the horror, the distress.

With heavenly artistry you touched our souls.

May joyous spiritual grace now make you whole.

WHITNEY HOUSTON

I had written about Whitney Houston for various outfits. I knew she was troubled. Issues rose in her life, then were quelled, covered by family and Houston herself. Too many prying eyes...too many envious hearts.

But if there were warning signs, only Whitney Houston could have realized what was happening. It is not for others to judge; it is impossible for others to know. We can only try to stand in another's shoes. And if we believe in the Lord, which Houston and her family surely did and do, then we must trust Him. Only He knows the purpose of our lives. He is the author and finisher of our faith. And the world may wag on, but He is the designer, and glory comes to Him through us.

That said, I've written this sonnet in remembrance of a beautiful and glorious child of God. He blessed her with his precious gifts. They will be treasured in our lifetime and beyond, because it is His joy to celebrate the goodness that shined the light of Whitney Houston.

WHITNEY HOUSTON

When you were born God's plan was set in place;

Your being not your own, the Tree of Life

Did hold you up and lift you to God's grace,

Though storms did try to beat you with their strife.

Though worldly, carnal lures would swallow you,

Though fame and fortune waved their glittery hands

And beckoned you embrace them as "the truth,"

And follow them in snares of their commands,

But never did the Lord allow your fall.

And never did you end your hope in God.

And never did you spurn the power of

Deliverance of the Light the world did trod.

With Christ in Spirit Whitney, live in Grace.

The Spirit softly holds you in Love's embrace.

MIKE NICHOLS

I remember Mike Nichols and Elaine May as a kid. They were a hysterical, witty, vibrant comedy team. I missed Nichols' Barefoot in the Park on Broadway, his first outing. The production helped to put Robert Redford on the map and was the first of his truly innovative and memorable collaborations with Neil Simon. Mike Nichols' direction of Edward Albee's Who's Afraid of Virginia Woolf and The Graduate identified him as a phenomenal, award-winning film director. I have seen most of his films and much of his most recent work on Broadway, including his fabulous Death of a Salesman for which he won his 8th Tony Award. Nichols is one of the few entertainers to have won the EGOT: the Emmy, Grammy, Oscar, and Tony. His award-winning legacy in all mediums makes one's head spin.

I had the opportunity to speak to Nichols at a performance of Betrayal which he directed. I was compelled to go over to him and state, "God Bless you for your work and what you have contributed." I sounded like an idiot stating that he had "made a difference" in my life. I saw him again at a performance of Twelfth Night. It was right after Philip Seymour Hoffman died. Mark Rylance spoke and there was a moment of silence for Hoffman, and it was just awful. Nichols was obviously suffering as were all in the theatre and film community.

Nichols was an amazing talent, a genius who sparked us to life and made us forget the monsters we were...for an hour or two or three as we laughed at his comedies (The Birdcage) or cried or mourned ourselves (Death of a Salesman). He made his art look easy and reminded us of what could be accomplished, despite economic woes and the grumblings of the profit-hungry about barely breaking even. Nichols, your value is beyond measure. Thanks for the truth and hope and energy of self. We are better for your having been in the world.

MIKE NICHOLS

Of platinum character and brilliant mind,

You forged a path no one but you could make:

Courageous artistry one-of-a-kind,

A determined will, no studio could break.

Elucidating themes of life for us

Reflecting hope, highlighting human flaws

With wisdom, clarity, acumen's trust.

Your films and plays and works? You gave us pause.

Your legacy's a beacon: we turn away

From vapid, puerile, soulless media fare

That Philistines present; the empty arts-

Are lacking substance, draining truth and care.

Your spiritual gifts and talents do inspire

Us to rekindle ancient drama's fires.

PETER O'TOOLE

I adore Peter O'Toole's work. As a kid I first saw him in Lawrence of Arabia. It was a wondrous film. It is still one of my favorites because of his and Omar Sharif's iconic performances. The brilliant direction of Sir David Lean, screenplay by Robert Bolt and Michael Wilson with Maurice Jarre's phenomenal music providing the glory to accompany the amazing cinematography, need no additional discussion. Deservedly winning 7 Oscars, the film's artistry is ineffable and incomparable. For me in its ethereality it represents the human soul, bleak, bare and beautiful.

The film resonated then, resonates now and will for all time. When we watch it, we are seeing age old issues related to defining identity and our abject inability to reign in our ungovernable natures. The film highlighted issues in the Middle East that are vital today: the politics of subtle imperialism and the easy bloodshed fomented by internecine conflicts.

Yet, O'Toole did not want to be associated with the role and for years selected parts that would take him out of the shadow of Lawrence. In an O'Toole biography I read, it was said he thought that his Masada role of Lucius Flavius Silva would finally free him from Lawrence. It did not because his Lawrence was a performance for the ages. In later years, he grew to appreciate the association with T.E. Lawrence and the unforgettable journey of the film which changed his life.

O'Toole was a great actor who could never be typecast. In each role, he wore the cloak of the character, looked out through the character's eyes, swallowed the saliva of the character, walked in his shoes, or at least, did with the characters in his finest, award nominated performances: The Stunt Man, The Ruling Class, My Favorite Year, The Creator, Becket, The Lion in Winter and even in Foxtrot. He was as acute an actor in his later work; I remember a BBC production in which he was frighteningly evil: The Dark Angel, aka Uncle Silas. He reached into the depths of humankind's wickedness and was its embodiment. Truly, it is an amazing performance. Of course, his role in Venus, for which he received his last Oscar nomination (nominated 8 times, he won an Honorary Oscar in 2003) was impeccable. O'Toole was nominated for and won many awards (BAFTA, Golden Globe,

Prime Time Emmy, Grammy etc.) throughout the 50 years of his career on stage, screen and in television.

This sonnet is from me to Peter, who referred to himself as a retired Christian. God loves the creative genius of artists which He fashions and encourages. In the finest artistry, we see His face in ours. If we allow Him to speak through us, as you did, Peter, then He and you are in a state of felicity. For surely, you are one of His bad boy darlings.

> A feisty Irishman an actor King,
>
> You were in life. Beloved for your art.
>
> You worshiped Shakespeare, did the classics bring
>
> To understanding roles, with a poet's heart.
>
> Your intellect self-schooled, and RADA trained,
>
> Evolved beyond the cares of Corn Flake men. *
>
> You scorned commercial "art." It diminished brains,
>
> And trashed humanity's worth, not of your ken.
>
> Your quality of spirit and your grace,
>
> Were known by family and a loving few.
>
> Your self-destructive threads and sorrowful traits
>
> Revealed. That knowing, you to you stayed true.
>
> Your gracious love shines out in graceful art,
>
> Remembered, lifted up. God's blessed, you, hart.

---

*Corn Flake men was O'Toole's reference to the CEOs of corporations who owned the studios and took over funding for films.

GORE VIDAL

Gore Vidal was an intellectual, political thinker of the 20th and beginning 21st century. To get a handle on the greatness of the patrician who advocated for the "little people," and Democracy, see the film Gore Vidal: The United States of Amnesia directed by Nicholas Wrathall.

Originally, this sonnet appeared on my website A Christian Apologist's Sonnets which Vidal would have chuckled to see, since he was an avowed atheist. On the other hand, Vidal was intellectually honest, heroic, brilliant and more representative of Jesus than most religious politicos who profess Christianity and live like Satanist hypocrites behind closed doors as they allow misogyny, racism, xenophobia, and other malevolences to rule their hearts.

Faux Christianity's message of the prosperity gospel ignores the Bible's "love of money is the root of all evil" ethic. Christian politicos place profits above people, gain votes and dupe the "stupid, unintellectual Christians who don't read or think." If we rightly divide truth from a lie, we can see seducing devils who would deceive Christ's very elect. Vidal could see. He was a prophet of the age. He transcended a brainwashed, white supremacist culture and defied labels, and stereotypes. So did Christ.

GORE VIDAL

Acerbic, vitriolic, searing words,

In you fermented, then poured out, a draught

Of wine. We sipped refreshed, the wisdom heard.

It quenched our ravaged souls and spirits wrought.

We culturally dispossessed? You raised us high.

Redeemed our history's worth with wit and grace,

And literary gifts none could decry.

Your genius ne'r could Truman* er' displace.

Self-described emotionally cold were you.

Patrician, righteous, prophet of the age,

To Buckley calumnious, to Mailer crude,

Tiresias: forthright, just, a humorous sage.

Your writings soar, though Death choked off your time.

You lived a maverick's life, one-of-a-kind.

Truman Capote. Vidal and Capote often knifed each other's work or person with serrated sarcasm.

TONI MORRISON

I taught African American Literature in a multicultural school district on Long Island years ago. We read Toni Morrison's novels, The Bluest Eye, Beloved and Song of Solomon after doing a unit on her life and groundbreaking work. We also watched Oprah Winfrey's amazing performance in Beloved, which is a marvelous, shattering film that did not receive the acclaim that it should have.

Morrison, a maverick, represents everything wonderful about the Black foundations of American history which she chronicles like no other American. She is a national treasure, opaque and mysterious to some, a dangerous spirit to others. That she is considered a blasphemy by craven GOP opportunists who would ban her books advocating the politically concocted bête noire, "critical race theory" makes me laugh. Her revelations about the cumulative noxious effects of American slavery on black and white culture are non-pareil.

It is dangerous not to read her, to ban her. Such censorship belies an inability to change and correct the hate-filled, genocidal, suicidal, white supremacist past. White supremacist racists support the "Big Brother" philosophy espoused in George Orwell's 1984, that history is made up and revised as needed; that wide swaths of it must be condemned or eliminated. Indeed, white supremacists have and continue to wipe out the facts about the Civil War and the aftermath of Reconstruction to further the oppressions and unconstitutional injustices the federal government and citizenry worked and voted to end. Not to wish to understand or acknowledge the history of the country one is a citizen of is a self-destructive and hate-filled blindness.

The beauty of Toni Morrison's writing is her empathy, shared humanity and encouragement toward redemption. All of us craven and intellectual need to sit at her feet and read her works. They are filled with jeweled riches that tell us about who we are, who we are capable of being and who we must become to help our country survive as a viable Democracy whose diverse populace accepts compromise to guarantee equality for oneself. This is particularly so in the midst of an assault engineered by conspiring monied cabals who despise equality and presume money gives them privilege to oppress to get what they alone want. These, who worship the Golden Calf and "love" money wear the appearance of populist Christianity but lack the power of the Spirit of Christ. Using politics and foreign dark money to push their own agenda, they would destroy the diversity that would strengthen our culture. Slavery was the epitome of such destruction. Morrison's work unveils this and inspires our society to grow up and redeem ourselves

You blew apart the shibboleths of white men,

Struck down the "white gaze" writers black did use,

Embraced with courage and love all human friends,

Struck down sadistic sickness of racism's abuse.

Through revelation your characters authentic, real.

Your stories of Black Americans' history,

Uplifted their sacred place racists would steal,

Through political power pawns' inhumanity.

How blessed your gifts, your talents God bestowed,

To comfort, enlighten, anger, redeem our souls,

Affirm our human nature empathetic. Unload

Our hurt and pain in stories; you broke the mold.

Your greatness, the Nobel Prize a token of

Your gracious heart revealed in Christ's pure love.

LEYNA GABRIELE

Leyna Gabriele was my maternal first cousin. She was the matriarch of our huge family after my mom and aunts and uncles of the first generations passed into spirit. She could be incredibly generous, loving, encouraging and kind. And she could be a Diva. Life with Leyna was an adventure of emotional highs and lows. For her nieces and nephews and their children she was a veritable Auntie Mame. A maverick bringing together opera and method acting with close friend and director Walt Witcover, she was a sensitive artist. Both Walt and Leyna brooked the Philistines of commercialism. In another time, apart from cultural misogyny and xenophobia, which she never admitted impacted her, oh what star.

Leyna was an opera singer of some renowned, having worked with composers Douglas Moore on The Ballad of Baby Doe because of her silvery soprano coloratura. Fans (The Doeheads) of Moore, Leyna and the opera adored her and would get together when the opera was presented. She also worked with John Kander testing out his compositions before he was part of the duo of Kander and Ebb. And she helped Jack Beeson work on his opera Hello Out There.

When Leyna became more established in New York City, she sang at Chez Vito, an exclusive supper club which featured opera singers like Cesare Siepe and others who sang at The Met, all dear friends. Owner Vito Pisa, whom Leyna married, produced two albums, A Night at Chez Vito and The Three Musketeers of the Opera at Chez Vito. Leyna was featured on both albums and family received copies. In its heyday Chez Vito was a celebrity magnet and high on the list of places to be seen around New York City. Leyna chilled with Werner von Braun, Nixon, Alfred Hitchcock (my brother Gabe could do a spot-on imitation of HItchcock at 8-years old) ZaZa Gabor, Gene Kelly, Joan Sutherland and Placido Domingo to name a few. She said Nixon had the mind of a steel trap.

An excellent voice teacher in later life, her students loved her. Leyna, who studied with Walt Witcover at HB Studios, was a superb acting teacher. She assisted opera singers in their interpretation of parts when their directors faltered. She shepherded them and gave them acting tips that made their performances believable and real, while maintaining voice control in the emotional sections. She and Walt Witcover presented La Traviata at Lee Strasberg's Actor's Studio, starring Leyna that has been credited in publications. The creative team effected a breathtaking, authentic production.

Miss you, Leyna. We all do. When you left us, you inspired me to finish my novel, Peregrine. Thanks for all of it, the good times, sad times, and enlightening revelations. Baci and abbracci.

      All beauty, glamor, striking majesty,

      You shined on paths you walked through light and dark.

      And people noted, turned to look and see

      Who was this presence bold, brave, vibrant, stark.

      Most gracious, kind and loving with your kin

      And friends alike who visited from afar,

      But your competitive spirit's ambition to win

      Was gracefully tempered not to be a star.

      Though star you were when we beheld your face,

      As youngsters Gabe and I admired you.

      We felt your impact on our lives. Your Grace

      Bestowed with laughter and Light what's real and true.

      Oh Leyna, I pray God's loving arms will keep,

      You safe, secure in New Life. Rest in Peace.

CICELY TYSON

The first time I ever saw Cicely Tyson, she portrayed Rebecca Morgan in Sounder (1972). Her performance was heartfelt, astounding and deserving of an Academy Award. She was nominated with fellow actress Diana Ross for Lady Sings the Blues. Both did not win. Twenty-nine years would pass before a black woman won a Best Actress Oscar: Halle Berry for Monster's Ball (2001). No actress has won since, though seven have been nominated. Such was the discrimination and white privilege that Cicely Tyson and other superlative black actresses were up against in Hollywood and the Studio System which prided itself on being "liberal." Things have not changed much. It is an understatement that they need to.

Cicely Tyson was known for her dignity in only selecting roles that were representative of honorable human beings and strong black women. Each time I saw her performances, whether it was in The Autobiography of Miss Jane Pitman (1974) the miniseries Roots (1977) or on Broadway in The Trip to Bountiful (2013) and The Gin Game (2015) with James Earl Jones, she was vibrant, elegant, and mesmerizing. She died at 95 during the COVID-19 time in January 2021. Her determination and personal power are beacons for all women and of special, particular significance to black women, triumphant.

CICELY TYSON

Stalwart, religious, faithful you carved your soul,

From living gemstones prism faceted light,

Dividing in rainbow colors, beauteous control.

Your presence emblematic of freedom's fight.

Mighty, iconic our leaders awarded you

With finest encomiums bestowed for all to see.

The younger ones you mentored. Always true,

You forged a path through mountainous bigotry.

Showed all who'd break through racism's iron doors,

A way of being in Christ that verified,

Your power as you remained on freedom's shores.

Your inner truth so purely justified.

Your indelible worth to walk at dear Christ's side.

We honor you as you walk in eternity's tides.

TERRANCE MCNALLY

Terrance McNally, whose career spanned six decades, was a master playwright of the dramatic and comedic. He also was a librettist and a screenwriter. His works were intensely, poetically, poignantly human. A five-time Tony winner (Love! Valor! Compassion! Master Class, The Kiss of the Spider Woman, Ragtime, Tony Lifetime Achievement Award in 2019) with four Drama Desks, two Lucille Lortels, two Obies, two Guggenheim Fellowships, a Rockefeller grant and Lifetime Achievement awards from Dramatists Guild and Lucille Lortel, he also won an Emmy.

More accolades included being inducted into the American Theater Hall of Fame and the highest honor that can be bestowed in the U.S: he was inducted into The American Academy of Arts and Letters. No wonder that he has been heralded as "one of the greatest contemporary playwrights the theater world has yet produced."

He was an incredible human being; an activist for gay rights early on when it was unfashionable even dangerous. He championed the craft of the playwright, holding the vice- presidency of the Council of the Dramatists Guild from 1981-2001.

Advocating for maverick, original, inclusive theater, McNally spoke to the League of American Theatres and Producers about the intention and mission of theater. He said, "I think theatre teaches us who we are, what our society is, where we are going. I don't think theatre can solve the problems of a society, nor should it be expected to...plays don't do that. People do. [But plays can] provide a forum for the ideas and feelings that can lead a society to decide to heal and change itself."

I saw/reviewed the superb documentary Every Act of Life at Tribeca Film Festival 2018. Afterward, there was a talk back with Terrance McNally, Nathan Lane, F. Murray Abraham, Joe Mantello and Tyne Daly about McNally, who said he never felt he was a playwright until about 6 years ago (2012) and this despite all his accolades. The film outlined how his artistry and authenticity contributed to his greatness.

Later that year, at the intermission of the fun Sponge Bob Square Pants, I could not resist going up to McNally, who was standing on the aisle. He must have thought I was insane when I rubbed his hand and said, "I hope some of you will rub off on me." He looked at me and smiled. I confessed I was a playwright and afraid to be produced. Kindly, he advised, "You can't be afraid." He told me that I had to hear my plays read aloud. He suggested that I invite friends over and have readings with pizza and beer to gauge what worked and what did not. I thanked him profusely. He was so incredibly kind and generous.

McNally had gone through rough periods in his life. He overcame alcoholism and illness. When I heard he contracted COVID and died in Sarasota, Florida, I was devastated. To me he was still a youngster at 81-years old. We were blessed with his presence and his wonderful plays, able to receive his sage wisdom, as he gave voice to issues about ourselves, society, and community.

Intensely kind, authentic, sensitive!

Your characters, in plays produced and staged,

Inhabited by actors who there lived.

Your words redeemed us from this current age.

Revealed, you mentored us in how to cope.

Revealed, the fear of AIDS and broken souls,

Whose lives so battered, deadened scouring hope,

Near lifeless, purposeless without control.

Your plays' transcendent moments transformed Light

From Dark, carved truth for your plays' themes.

We understood from you that we must fight,

In heartache's trials must love, ourselves redeem.

To be in greatness, we must live in Grace,

Circling in peace and wholeness, Love embraced.

REQUIEM FOR EDGAR ALLAN POE

Edgar Allan Poe married his cousin Virginia Clemm when she was 13 and he was 27. Whether her immune system was weakened from the stresses of the marriage and Poe's rumored philandering, which devastated her, Virginia Eliza Clemm contracted tuberculosis and withered for 5 years until she died. On her deathbed, she accused the woman with whom Poe allegedly had an affair as being indirectly responsible for her death. Poe never forgave himself. He was wracked by guilt, though he attempted to expiate this through his writings and poems like Annabel Lee, The Raven, and Ulalume.

The stress and burden of this guilt, the anxiety of attempting to make a successful writing career, and his endeavors to land a marriage with a wealthy women consumed him as did alcoholic binges and mysterious illnesses. He was found lying in a Baltimore gutter delirious and under great duress. Transported to Washington Medical College where he died four days later, his cause of death was occluded; the truth has yet to materialize. The mysteries that he had confronted during his lifetime brought him to an early and lonely end. Along with his brilliant, unparalleled poems, criticisms, novels and short stories, this mystery infuses his ethos with Gothic Romance and adds to the mystique of one of the grandest and most globally beloved of American writers. My two-act play Edgar is dedicated to Poe.

REQUIEM FOR EDGAR ALLAN POE

The mysteries of the world they are writ large

Upon your soul as deep as darkness' sea.

Your prescient being over wrought and charged

With quantifying consciousness. To free

Your loving cousin to communicate

In ethers, time warps, stretching toward the stars,

Bending spirits aligned to altered states,

You'd bring her close to you who was so far.

The gulf of death you crossed; scorned mortal shores.

Alone upon the waves of time and light,

You drove your words and thoughts and hope restored,

Continued through life's hellish days and nights.

And then your soul's cruel wanderings did cease.

Joined with your love eternal in Christ's peace.

POLITICS AND RELIGION

‡

A PRAYER FOR NATIONAL RECONCILIATION

Oh Lord bring Light into political hearts!

Convict them of their lying, murderous ways,

And thwart their lust for money. Help them part

From lobbyist's seductions, their oaths betray.

Make strong intentions to our lives protect,

And stir them to their mission in unity,

To help the helpless who institutions neglect,

And sacrifice in Sadism's treachery.

Oh Lord expose those who refuse to bow

To Love and Hope and Grace and Truth and Faith.

And open the eyes of followers and those they con,

And use because they deem them human waste.

Lord unify with Love the True and Just,

To help those who Politicos treat as dust.

THE GOLDEN CALF AND MAMMON
The Lust of the Flesh, The Lust of the Eye, The Pride of Life

When Moses left the Israelites with Aaron to converse with God on Mount Sinai, they had a crisis of faith. Many complained against Moses and the God who delivered them with miracles from Pharoah's soldiers. They forgot how the Angel of Death destroyed the first born in Egypt. They dismissed God's supernatural power, that not even the magicians of Egypt could duplicate.

Materialistic, carnal, the Israelites replaced God's love with a god they could see, a golden calf which they worshiped. The same abides for us today when we take our eyes off the spiritual things of God and only concern ourselves with material riches. When Christ said, "Blessed are they who believe and do not see," he was identifying the greatness of faith that depends not on the five senses, or the material realm or the physical world. Spiritual faith that is the substance of things hoped for, the evidence of things NOT SEEN is life fulfilling. The message-tie-in is clear. Worshiping material objects brings misery, torment, unhappiness. And these emotions lead to self-destruction. Cupidity is a terrorist of the soul, along with the lust of the eyes, the pride of life and the hungers of obsessive passion for people or things. Obsessions never satisfy. Only spiritual wisdom brings peace and makes us whole.

THE GOLDEN CALF AND MAMMON

The pride of life Christ warns brings fear and doubt,

Dispels one's trust in God and Holy things,

And drains one's hope, creates a spiritual drought,

Kills expectations that God's blessing brings.

Renewal, wholeness, peace, the majesty,

To seal one's purpose vibrant light and life,

Can never be ransomed from cupidity.

And covetous lust does darken Christ's pure light.

Those who are blind and deaf and dumb to God,

The mighty acts unseen in bloated lives,

Do manifest the lust of flesh and trod,

The seeds of Faith and Truth. Christ's love denied.

Oh Lord! Bestow your mercy! Rent the veil,

That cloaks such souls in darkness. Let love prevail!

CHRIST'S LAW OF LOVE: A WOMAN'S RIGHT TO CHOOSE

This is a sonnet dedicated to all the women who have sacrificed their lives and died giving themselves an illegal abortion. They chose to take possession of their souls and bodies regardless of the political culture's anti-Christian laws, denying them safe healthcare with a medical doctor. Christ said God's commandments are encompassed in the first two: 1) Love God with all your heart, soul, mind, strength (the joy of the Lord is your strength) 2) Love your neighbor as yourself.

Politics is not God. Pro-lifers are being used by politicos to obtain voting power. There is nothing Christian about such politics. They go against God's scriptures and with politicos blaspheme the Holy Spirit and lie on His Word.

Exodus 21: 22-23 makes it clear that a dependent life (fetus) does not have the same value as an independent life. If they were equivalent, all the women who have lost their children through natural abortions (i.e. ectopic pregnancy) are murderers and should get the death penalty. Either the woman and fetus are separate, independent beings, or one is an independent being and one is a dependent being. Exodus 21: 22-23 indicates the fetus is dependent. The mother's life is independent. Thus, if a man causes a pregnant woman to miscarry and the child dies, he is fined, but only if the woman lives. If he causes the woman to miscarry and she dies with the fetus, then he is charged with murder.

CHRIST'S LAW OF LOVE: A WOMAN'S RIGHT TO CHOOSE

Because you're born a woman you are trapped

Inside a female body. You're oppressed

By those who hate. Your power they would sap,

To dominate what God has truly blessed.

The patriarchy spirit is a lie,

That masquerades as truth, a fearful threat.

It harms and maims and kills those who would try,

To overthrow its legion of regrets.

Conservatives, mountebanks-quotidian whores,

These hypocrites use "Christian" politics.

In shadows they belie Christ is the door.

They practice not God's love, but Satan's tricks.

Women's souls are free, their choices, rights,

Dear Christ has granted as a sacrifice.

GALILEO GALILEI AND GOD

Oh Galileo! Did you not "make waves?"

The Catholic Church would burn you at the stake.

But you profoundly studied 'til your grave,

Though fearful cardinals would your soul to break.

A physicist! The foremost of the times!

You disobeyed, like Paul, and traveled to

Old Tuscany to preach the heavens' rhymes,

In concepts blasphemous to monkish "truth."

Those scribes, those pharisees in spirit like

The same who crucified The Son of Man

Could never justify their devilish strike,

Against God's great astronomer and stand.

The One whose physics tamed The Galilee*

Displaced the carnal church through Galilei.**

---

*Many of Christ's greatest miracles happened at or around the Lake of Galilee: feeding the 5,000, calming the storm that frightened the disciples, walking on the water to Peter who went out of the boat to join Him, lost faith and was sinking. There Christ taught the disciples to be "fishers of men."
**Galileo's last name

TO UNIFY THE NATION

Our courage is not seen in Florida.

Traditions subtly bake confederate sons.

The stubborn static, not America.

Obduracy clouds what's true, what's right, what's won.

Hyperactive New York shortens time,

Redefines land-space into the air.

The globe, with New York City is aligned.

Times Square the polyglot beyond compare.

Invigorating, crisp with energy,

The Northern East Coast sings its siren's song.

Stirs youth to seek Manhattan's majesty.

Success? Dynamic efforts must be strong!

Confederate hatreds harm the national will.

Oh God, guide us to love; our destiny fulfill.

BLACK LIVES MATTER

I have no words except to affirm the title of this sonnet. Immigrants, blacks who were brought here against their will in 1619 and "freed" by the Emancipation Proclamation (save the Texans' horror to egregiously keep blacks in the dark about their freedom until Juneteenth) have uplifted this nation with their fight for their constitutional rights. They and Native Americans are in an exalted position above all of us, for they founded this nation. Rights are power. Any group or person attempting to curtail anyone else's rights via demeaning behavior, whose ultimate intent is to remove their identity and being, is a murderer and should seek peace in Christ and repent. (for Christians, that is against commandments 1 and 2). Ultimately, such self-hatred ends in a failed, miserable, self-destructive life.

There is no excuse for hating someone who is different, for all of us are different. To disdain why Colin Kaepernick protested police brutality by taking a knee during the National Anthem is to disdain the Bill of Rights in the First Amendment of the Constitution. We may protest unjust behavior, for example unequal justice under the law and the brutality of the police who have killed black men and women for no good reason and have gotten away with it. Such killings are tantamount to lynchings. To refuse to examine the history of lynching out of arrogance and blatant racism by saying that's "critical race theory" is to belie the truth.

The history of The White League, the KKK, the Aryan Nation, the Neo Nazis and other white supremacist hate groups that have spilled out into the culture today is not theory. It is fact. There is nothing theoretical about racism. Racism is one way to make money and gain power via a class of individuals who divide and conquer. Oftentimes, the law has been used to oppress anyone who was not a white male. That power structure is exposed as destructive and self-hating. Slowly, love is conquering it.

One cannot truly say one is a citizen of this nation unless one understands that civil rights and patriotism are about upholding constitutional law, not abusing the law to destroy others in a hate crime. To counter the statement "Black Lives Matter" with the phrase, "All Lives Matter" ignores that vast numbers of black men and women were lynched, burned alive, jailed falsely, abused and starved. We can't change our history. But we can change our hearts that would ignore or condone past hatreds.

Let's be honest. If one is a white supremacist and a killer, one should have the courage to admit it. Then to you, "black lives don't matter." Well, in this nation, you are a tiny percentage belonging to an outcast tribe. Would that you repent and turn from murder in your heart. Only then can you say that "All Lives Matter." Only then will you believe that you and everyone else matters.

> Reflecting on the trials of history,
> I can't forgive our treacherous, bloody past:
> The sacrificial hanged on Justice's tree
> To foster a Southern confederate's sweet repast.
> Denounced the debauchery of inhuman needs
> To chain another, make them do slave work;
> Mistreat them, starve, demean them for their greed,
> Because in leisurely life they labor shirked.
> That time is done? Oh no! In this "free" land,
> Are traitors who uplift such murderous will.
> In arrogance decry us as we stand,
> Against such murders. Can't break us, make us still!
> Exposed the Spirit of Evil. Christ casts them down.
> The righteous unify; the hate-filled drown.

THE SPIRIT OF HYPOCRISY

All of us are hypocrites, and stone throwers. "Let he who is without sin cast the first stone." We fail and we throw stones, criticize others for what we despise in ourselves. However, there is always the hope to reverse, to correct, to grow, to evolve away from addictive behaviors: self-hatred, unforgiveness, anger, pride, impatience, unkindness, ignorance, narcissism. Those are true malevolences. Addictions like overeating, alcoholism, opioid, or heroin addiction are the symptoms of soul problems.

Some individuals resolve to be kinder, gentler persons and check themselves constantly for hypocrisy. However, how is one kind to an abusive bully who sees "kindness" as weakness? Christ said, "Turn the other cheek." I interpret this to address the bully, "If it will make you feel better, slap me on this other cheek even harder this time, so you can feel better and stop your obvious misery. Your emotional needs are more important than mine." But these comments must be said with power, truth, sincerity and conviction, the type of conviction and unction with which Christ spoke. That is with the anointing of the Living God.

THE SPIRIT OF HYPOCRISY

Oh Lord, you reign in wisdom, love and grace.

Provide us strength when cares we place on you.

The meek, the poor, the patient see your face,

Accept your powerful faith and live in Truth.

And those of Spiritual faith? They occupy,

Wait as you shine your brilliance, manifest

Your truth and facts, that hypocrites despise,

Call fake while soul torments bring their unrest.

To live a life unmired by self-hate,

To live with peace, good will toward all in love,

Requires courage, righteousness and faith,

That overtakes our souls through Christ's sweet dove.

Oh, Mighty Christ dethrone the Hypocrite!

Cast down that spirit in power. Help us resist.

JUSTICE, RIGHTS, FREEDOM: IN THE NAME OF GOD!

At the time (2013) Edward Snowden turned the world upside down. We still do not understand what happened there. Did leaders turn ethics upside down? Is black-white, truth-a lie, heroism-betrayal? Who are the traitors and who are the heroes? What are our rights anyway when you have no rights the moment you walk into your employer's building?

Who does one stand with if one's government has violated its own laws and then denies it as the Trump Administration did daily? What do those who "spill the beans," so to speak, have to gain? All is muddied water. Clarity is needed. But what if you are born in a time without being able to see truth, a time when ethics don't really hold much sway, when success, power and money are the God to worship? What do you do if those who profess to be looking out for and praying for humanity (Christians) are lost in the abyss, following blind politicos who profess Christianity but live like devils?

Christ said, "The blind lead the blind and they all fall in the ditch." In the land of the blind, the one-eyed man is king. One must discern truth from a lie; Christ protects his elect, so they are not deceived.

JUSTICE, RIGHTS, FREEDOM: IN THE NAME OF GOD!

Oh Christ, I cannot fathom all your ways.

When those parade your name and speak of peace,

Yet war they bring for profit. Then betray

The ones who fight, who die, who pray surcease.

Oh do you listen to these war lords when,

They pray increase to all their treasuries?

Oh do you grant them happiness, defend

Them from opponents and their enemies?

Those who uphold our freedoms and our rights,

The tyrants see as chaff to be destroyed.

They call them traitors, see them as a blight

On global plans elite groups have deployed.

Oh God of righteousness is justice slain?

Help us return to justice in Your Name.

C.S. LEWIS AND AGAPE LOVE

In C.S. Lewis' brilliant The Four Loves, the author discusses the greatest love, agape, which is Christ's love for us. It entails sacrifice, giving one's life for another. It is a spiritual, divine, and all-encompassing love. It is given freely with no expectation of return. This is the "turn the other cheek love." It is impossible unless one is in Christ's spirit and renewing one's mind in the Word daily.

From the perspective of individuals on the receiving end, if they are not in Christ's spiritual adulthood, often they do not realize what it is. Such love is incomprehensible to the human mind. All manner of twisting and distortion occurs about it, until finally the anointing breaks through (probably years later) and the understanding comes to the one on the receiving end. Most likely, the individual giving the agape, and the "receptor" have long gone to other spheres of influence. As the Word says: the seed was planted, one came and watered, another tilled the soil around the plant, another provided the sustenance, etc.

This sonnet is representative of such agape love, which is spiritual and never physical. The closest thing to the physicality of agape is feeling inner peace, warmth, and forgiveness; it's power can send chills running up and down one's spine at its recognition and its presence. Being physical is so far beneath agape because it is mortal and selfish. Physicality can harm the power of agape love through objectification of another's soul, making it a nonentity (think what the Nazis did to eradicate self/identity in the concentration camps).

Agape is the greatest love because it leads to redemption and renewal of the soul in Christ. Agape defies logic. To the materialistic world, agape is foolish. But God takes the foolish things of the world to confound the wise.

C.S. LEWIS AND AGAPE LOVE

Oh Christians, Christ emboldened you with Love.

This Grace bestowed upon all chosen ones.

In hallowed sanctity of world's above

The carnal, worldly realms we surely shun.

And you, confounded, and perplexed, undone,

By that, you cannot seem to grasp or see,

Will learn in seasons ripe that you are One,

With Spirit in the Grace of unity.

A vessel or an ark, a ship so strong,

Christ's making of your soul to receive peace.

So don't throw off Christ's love; it is a song

To celebrate your freedom from sin's lease.

Just know this hymn of love envelopes you.

Christ's love and mine are One with you in truth.

WHEN MINDS ARE CLOSED

When minds are closed there is no way to start

The process where a soul is joined to Christ.

The head and heart have fully grown apart,

Can't be conjoined but for a heavy price.

I've crashed against the godless' jagged song,

That life is random circumstance confused,

That Death absurdly wipes away the strong,

Propounds humanity's purpose as refuse.

Such wanderers on earth will fallow lie

In isolation's shadows, torment's slaves.

Such darkened beings substanceless can't give.

They know not but to burrow in a grave.

Thus, soil and soul the evil worms do gnaw.

Condemned the godless* trapped in Satan's** maw.

Those separated from God-hypocrites and religious politicos
**The Spirit of arrogance, pride, condemnation of others, lies, denial*

UNITED STATES OF AMERICA

Within America does freedom ring?

Do bells of liberty bestow their wealth?

Or do the carnal ones in death-states sing,

And every fly and snake sting Christ in stealth?

Is freedom in our souls a foolish hope

To think about before one takes one's life?

Or is Christ's Light-Filled Truth beyond earth's scope,

Achieved when golden* peace reigns without strife?

Is Truth ephemeral, not common sense,

A bloody lie, a doctrine of false thought?

Or is its power so great and so intense,

It's known the moment we see its Light is wrought?

Christ's Freedom, Liberty and Truth come forth,

So we can see the Glory of the Lord.

*golden: full of divine nature

POLITICAL ARROGANCE

Politicos, deceit has eaten you,

Destroyed once loving, simple, peaceful hearts,

And forced your horrid hatreds to be truth,

And butchered sweet beginnings of God's art.

You're now those calloused beings weak and lamed,

By Satan's* grinning trickery and hate.

Your minds are festering wounds. And Evil's named

You to a destiny of cruel fate.

Your lies that tricked the nation, tricked you too,

In thinking you're above God's just, true eyes.

You lie that only QAnon is true,

Embracing treason, you yourselves, despise.

You've turned your back on Jesus' loving ways,

Entrapped yourselves in Satan's* dark decay.

*The Spirit of arrogance, pride, condemnation of others, lies, denial

TROLLS

This puppet's life of mind must come to end.

For I am done with being another's troll.

Like parasites on me they did depend,

And gladly did I yield, gave them control.

I took their hate-filled burdens on my heart,

Despised myself adjusting to their needs,

And when I tried to leave and from them part,

Their anger and offense off me did feed.

I learned to thrive conformed to their weird shape,

Grotesque and monstrous, saprophytic, cruel.

I'd learned to obviate my sickly state,

Enthralled, ensnared to be their wicked fool.

I call the Lord to cleanse my puppet's soul,

And free my mind from their sadistic hold.

A POLITICIAN'S HARD REDEMPTION

It matters not what you propose to do.

It matters not what you propose to stop.

Your actions in compendium untrue,

Convince you that you are what you are not.

The paradox of image in your mind,

Has overthrown reality's device,

Seduced you to assume your actions kind,

Although in truth they're cruelly steeped in lies.

And so for every word and deed performed,

For every smile and frown upon your face,

The deepest credibility foresworn

Is self-deception you will n'er erase.

Your ego is undone. Christ vanquished you.

The Light performed a miracle of Truth!

REDEEM OUR BETRAYAL OF OUR NATION
Group Prayer for Politicians Who Support "The Big Lie" *

The snake deceit coiled round our questing hearts,

And struck. Its venom streamed all through our souls.

In shock we slowly realized the part,

We played. Confused and conned we lost control.

We let the others' treason snare our brain,

That chafed our love of self, 'til bleeding raw,

We fell and let the blood-filled droplets drain,

To sate the infinite thirst of Satan's** maw.

That wicked spirit destroys the hope of those,

Who're lost in darkness, absent peace and faith.

For them who're blind, corruption does enclose

Their minds with cruelty, treachery, lies and hate.

Dear Christ! Deliver us from self-deceit.

Restore our faith, our nation, make whole, complete.

Trump lies saying he won the 2020 election. He lost in a landslide to President Biden
**The Spirit of arrogance, pride, condemnation of others, lies, denial*

THE CHURCH SEDUCTION

With worldliness the whore, the Church* seduced,

The chosen to believe that they were dung.

She bought and sold and toyed with them and used,

Their true Christ worth. As heroes; they're unsung.

False Church, the Harlot tricked Saints so naive.

Behind their backs she trod Christ's spiritual blood,

Played holy to convince them to believe

Her lies were truth: Hell's noxious, demonic flood.

Then God unleashed His powers to conquer her,

Through Chosen Ones who worked to overtake

Her wicked kingdom. And He greatly stirred

Those who're seduced that saw what was at stake.

Oh Christ! The Church's whoredoms You exposed.

With light and love you saved The Elect you chose.

Mystery Babylon the Mother of Harlots (Revelation 17: 5) using religious fervor to create cult worship

REVOCATION OF THE UNAPOLOGETIC

The revocation of Christ's fruitful Love,

Lays like a futile branch, rot-soaked in rain,

Whose life once vibrant reached for skies above,

But now, chopped off, laid waste, the fire's gain.

The bark stripped black is melted in white fires,

And it becomes grey ash amending earth.

Then insects syphon xylem's liquid spires

And dissipate once strong and beauteous worth.

Surrounding me the fields refuse display,

And timber's members wrenched from vital trees,

Lay lifeless, strewn promiscuous in decay,

Like ships storm torn, rock gouged, sea swept, off lead.

Oh Savior! Ne'r revoke Your Love from me.

Abide always within, whole, fruitful, free.

TRADE MARKET

There is no market for the sensitive.

Consumerist society is crass,

And meretricious in the way we live,

Devoid of culture's art and sacred past.

The wealthy make politicos keep this state,

As if the beastly poor'd despoil them.

The misery they cause with classist hate

Does strangle hope and would our lives to end.

To buy and sell your soul they'd make us dead.

Both rich and poor are caught in Mammon's grasp.

And all are pushed and forced to "get ahead,"

Then wallow in the dust, ripe for Death's clasp.

The saints and poets, sensitive and True,

Cannot be bought or sold, nor me, nor you!

REQUITED LOVE IS CHRISTMAS

It doesn't matter whether you say Merry Christmas or don't. The Christmas message is clear and it's for everyone, regardless of your religion and especially for those who profess Christianity but hypocritically deny CHRIST'S POWER to overcome fear, guilt, hate and sorrow. The message is Christ's love and forgiveness. So, confess your pains and torments and guilt and shame to someone who cares for you, even if it's just yourself. And allow the perfection of Christ's Love to heal you and bring you peace for all time.

You'll never feel the sting of shame or hate.

You'll walk in comfort and in love's sweet peace.

The Christmas message overcomes your fate,

Extends your body's health and yearly lease.

The problem lies when troubles snare our mind,

And doubts take charge and snuff the light of Christ,

Then lower us to darkness and the grind

Of pain, that nullifies His sacrifice.

The cross is empty. All Christ's work is done.

So why allow depression and despair,

To break our hearts and never overcome,

The knowledge that our lives He did repair?

With love, forgiveness, hope the message's clear.

That Christmas reigns from year to year to year.

RESURRECTION AFTER COVID-19

COVID-19 has been a transformative cataclysm. In NYC I live 6 miles from the epicenter where people lined up waiting to get into the infamous Elmhurst Hospital in Queens and died. Because of the leadership of Governor Andrew Cuomo, that debacle of chaos and death was mitigated. He and his team's sanity and skills helped guide New Yorkers to follow his protocols, despite the botched, inhumane response of selfish Trump, accessorized by GOP leaders who made money off the pandemic. Trump cared more about reelection to escape prison, than the welfare of U.S. citizens.

I wrote this at the height of death and dying when New York had the highest infection rate in the world. Cuomo and New Yorkers brought the rate to the third lowest. New Yorkers applauded Governor Cuomo's leadership amidst the hell and despair brought by the Republican Party and Trump administration accountable for negligent heart murder. The Governor told us the truth about COVID'S dangers and led us to save our own lives and the lives of each other. If the GOP had followed his lead instead of smearing him, COVID would not have spread to "red" states and killed thousands; their numbers are still underreported. The unworthy party of denial and insurrection couldn't safeguard citizens' health. Judge Cuomo? Let he who is without sin cast the first stone. Begin with Donald Trump who called COVID-19 a hoax and the flu, though he knew of its lethal capabilities in January 2020.

The GOP and Republican Party are craven in pushing a political response to COVID, warring against citizens by not acknowledging the problem as a public health emergency. Many died obeying Trump/GOP lies, and they still die (August, 2021). The unvaccinated, following GOP conspiracy theories, vitiate their civic responsibility as citizens to protect each other. Duped by Putin and Russian Military Intel's war against the U.S. and democracy, QAnon followers uplift their individual right to kill themselves and take as many as possible with them. They are the weapons Putin provokes to destroy U.S. citizens. The GOP, for political purposes, stealthily promotes QAnon's fraudulent claims about the vaccine.

RESURRECTION AFTER COVID-19

Oh Christ, displace our country's hate and fear!

Please shed Your love upon all darkened hearts.

Anoint our leaders to through treachery steer

The ship of Nation-States to do their part.

Help them to recognize there's unity,

In helping hands despite divisiveness.

And guide them over shoals of treachery,

So they put first their citizens' distress.

And cheer our hearts with humor and with joy,

And show us hope and generosity.

Give leaders strength and mercy. You deploy

Forgiveness and redemption. Make us Free!

You are the resurrection and the Life.

Dispel the darkness. Shine Your brilliant Light.

SONNETS OF THE SOUL

SOUL TRIALS

I stand nearby a wide expanse of sea,

And watch a figure walking toward the shore.

It silent moves the waves as if so free.

I feel a magic drown the ocean's roar.

In all the monuments to men once great,

There is no one who speaks of love and grace,

That Christ does offer, though some despise and hate,

God's mercy when self-loathing is erased.

The ones who hate do bow their lives to men.

And claim that "mankind" does such wondrous things.

But monuments will tumble and what then,

For those who shunned, refused Christ's offerings?

As Christ comes near, His arms reach out to me.

I walk in Spiritual Faith on raging seas.

THE LOST PSYCHIATRIST

Right after my senior year in college, I turned my back on God. I went to a Freudian psychiatrist. For him it was all about psychic masochism and the teachings of Edmund Bergler, who had met Freud. Bergler created his own version of psychotherapy, which my psychiatrist followed for years. The therapy, which condemns gays, has since been discredited. My psychiatrist pushed homosexual conversion therapy, now banned in many U.S. states and provinces in Canada. I am not gay, nevertheless, the treatment did not help me or others. I remained depressed and felt hopeless that my life would never change.

Years later (1980) I saw him intermittently since his practice was in Toronto. He told me his own psychiatrist erred in the treatment, but he improved it. After sessions and experiencing his increased arrogance that he had cured himself, I realized that there was something amiss. Reading C.S. Lewis' wonderful books restored my faith in Christ and gave me a renewed strength and wisdom. I tried to share this with him, but we never had a dialogue of sensitive understanding. He did not respect me for who I was. When I challenged him, he refused to discuss why he bullied me to leave my husband who wouldn't see him for treatment. (He didn't give me sessions until I left my husband.) At the time I thought the only way for me to be at peace was through his Berglerian "cure." When I questioned why he was glad I had gotten a divorce and returned to treatment, he gave me an unsatisfying answer that my husband was harmful, and he didn't want me hurt.

My faith helped me realize that my husband was not the harmful one, the psychiatrist was. He abused my trust and lacked the one thing that is required of any therapist, compassion. Obeying my intuition, I left. Decades later, this psychiatrist was "de-licensed" because he sexually abused his gay patients. When I read about him, I had already gotten my Ph.D. By then I had worked through my rage at being psychically abused by this sick doctor. My Two-Act comedy, The Berglarian, a fiction, is inspired by what happened with him. This sonnet was written after I left treatment. (1982)

THE LOST PSYCHIATRIST

I think of you and wonder where you are

In fate's strange realm that weaves a lurid spell,

To charm you into nets that men throw far

To catch your soul in lies where you then dwell.

You slave and toil to satisfy your kin,

Who judge your worth by standards of the world,

That trods you down in guilt and acts of sin,

So, from your destiny you will be hurled.

But yet, in you there grows a light that's strong,

That burns to know the Truth and make you blind

In faith, which steers you from that which is wrong,

And guides you to God's wisdom, self-love then find.

The light is Christ who Darkness does abate.

It gives redemption, vanquishes self-hate.

SOUL STRUGGLE

During the time my faith was strengthening in God, and I was pulling away from the psychiatrist mentioned on the previous page, I suffered through depression, wondering if I had made the right decision. My writing, prayer and reading the Bible (Old and New Testament several times which I was familiar, with raised Baptist as a child) brought me into a place of gradual peace. From a calm state, I could make cogent decisions about my life. This occurred after I had a relationship with a filmmaker, I met at HB Studios where I studied acting. Acting was a passion I had as a child. This individual helped me get through the death of my X husband, the one the psychiatrist bullied me to leave or I would remain "uncured." The more I embraced and renewed my faith in God, the stronger my spirit and soul became.

Eventually, I went back to finish my Ph.D. and pursue a writing career. Most of the sonnets in this unit were composed in the 1980s during the time I was finding out who I was in Christ, what I wanted and what gave me peace. My sonnet "New Creation" was completed after the struggle when I was on solid ground with no shifting sands. Since then, my faith has continued to grow in Christ (not a political religious faith, but a spiritual one).

SOUL STRUGGLE

Oh, fight I must to keep my sanity,

In this dark time of horror, pain and dread.

Base forces pluck and tear and aim for me,

To plummet hope, make me believe I'm dead.

For resignation dwells within our hearts,

And eats away one's spirit, gifts, and dreams.

And resignation in one's soul will start

The life force down Death's horrid path of schemes.

I look around and notice souls alike,

Who resignation eats three times a day.

Such souls have died and could not lead a strike,

Against the brutal force of Satan's* way.

I have success through Christ's love and his Grace.

Fight spiritual battles, insure self-hate's erased.

**The Spirit of arrogance, pride, condemnation of others, lies, denial*

SHATTERING

There's something evil tearing at my soul,

That stalks the inmost tender part of me,

That rends the life force that creates my whole,

Then pounces on the weakest parts it sees.

It comes in pleasing shape, yet devilish eye,

Of one whose charm and grace encounters all

The girls who lack the self-esteem to try,

To lock away the urge to pitch and fall.

As evil whips up searing frailties,

A fault-line splits my being, growing strong.

So, I lash out in blind cupidity,

Toward kind souls who have done me no great wrong.

I look to God whose mercy leads the way,

Receive the Word that washes doubt away.

FLOATING

At times I lose perspective of God's plan,

For me in helping guide those to Love's fold.

I'm taken by the Devil's* hate of man/woman

And thus, I'm thwarted by a searing cold.

It permeates my soul and being full,

Flows into condemnation of myself.

From others' words and deeds, I'm easily pulled

Away to hatred, strife and sorrow's stealth.

How do I fight my imperfection, here?

Too weak am I to forego doubt-filled days!

How can I overcome my mammoth fears?

They stifle spirit, thrust me in Hell's** ways!

The answer comes. I triumph after all.

I seek Dear Christ who saves me from Hell's** thrall!

*The Spirit of arrogance, pride, condemnation of others, lies, denial
*doubt, fear, self-hate, torment, psychic pain, depression

MY LOVE OF GOD GROWS DEEPER EVERY DAY

My love of Christ grows deeper every day.

As I perceive the love for me in One,

Sent here to save us from Old Serpent's ways,

To offer heavenly kingdoms through God's Son.

I'm overwhelmed that Christ's selected me,

To join the hosts who worship at Christ's side.

For wicked deeds and actions, mine I see,

Not worthy of God's Kingdom to abide.

Yet, Christ forgives my flawed, corrupted life,

Finds value, beauty, joy within my soul,

Is willing to cleanse me of torment, strife,

Pluck me from condemnation's biting cold.

I bow to God with thankfulness and love,

Receiving Spiritual Truths, I'm worthy of.

SURCEASE

How fearful is my soul at my past life,

When Evil* lurked behind my every thought.

How knowledge of such actions caused my flight,

To dreams and hopes where spirit life is fraught

With love and mercy from One born to die,

Upon a cross to save our errant souls.

For humans deep in Hell's** despair can lie,

Condemned forever tortured. Satan's goal.

At times my darkened nature charges fast,

Upon my situation with my kin,

And grief and hopelessness are my repast,

Which make me feel I'm overwhelmed in sin.***

I look to Christ to calm my tortured mind.

In Spiritual Love I leave all cares behind.

---

*hate, self-hate, jealousy, doubt, fear, depression, self-condemnation, separation from God's love
**hell, evil, Satan are all of the same cloth, beginning with fear and doubt
***separation from God's love that we are worthy and forgiven

I FEEL MY CHRISTIAN SOUL

I feel my Christian soul retreat inside.

Vanadium doors block out true loving thoughts.

And shackled by a demon self I hide

From God and people's comfort I once sought.

How did this force deceitful assault me?

I thought prepared I'd been by love of self,

To conquer Satan's* wild seductive sprees

To cripple me and maim my mind with stealth.

I'm held within a vacuumed space and time,

Until My Savior burns those hellish doors.

I pray that once I'm freed my soul in rhyme,

Will walk in Spirit's artistry once more.

As I believe, Christ loves and mercy gives.

The doors melt down and once again I live.

*Spirit of arrogance, self destruction, jealousy, doubt, fear, depression, self-condemnation, separation from God's love (hell, evil, Satan are all of the same cloth)

SHAKING OFF DESPAIR

Here comes Despair, companion to myself.

My fallible declivities he treads.

Embracing me, he's mischievous as an elf.

He wheedles and cajoles me to his bed.

And there I lie with him in wanton lust,

Full bodied, for a revel, self-indulged.

Too sated, then I look to him to trust,

But find too late, too much I have divulged.

A snare I'd circled round myself with him.

A patterned repetition in my life.

Escape despair? A spark of hope begins,

To stop enjoying sorrow, pain and strife.

My axis turns and I turn toward the Lord.

Christ's Love momentum frees me. I move forward.

I WAKE TO FACE THE NIGHT

I wake to face the night-fell universe.

Dark space unleashed berefts me from selfhood.

In alienation conscience is accursed.

My being shattered, taunted by Hell's* brood.

My soul is pitch. No emanating light,

Flows out to bond with fellow human beings.

In shallowed tides I'm mired by Death's blight,

And resignation to soul's hapless gleanings.

Hot spears of guilt make black, hope's sustenance.

With accusations, devils** fill my heart,

Propel pain inward. Pierced with evil sense,

In tortuous tumult I betray my art.

A miracle! Christ's Love encircles me,

Electrifies my faith and spirit frees.

---

*Spirits of hate, self-hate, jealousy, doubt, fear, depression, self-condemnation, separation from God's love
**Spirits of depression, hopelessness, despair that would lead one to self-destruction

LAST NIGHT A SPECTRAL FIGURE

Last night a spectral figure kissed my hand,

Caressed my face with fiery, burning breath,

And beckoned me to follow on the strand,

Engaging me to join his Dance of Death.

In gross temptation I swayed to his side,

Unleashed unconsciousness to wander forth,

And slip toward Lethe wharf with him as guide,

A pawn to show God Satan's* cruel retort.

But jarred by circumstances, I awoke.

Confronted desolation's hoary face.

As car smashed curb, I swerved and wheel I broke.

I lived protected by Christ's loving Grace.

That night a warning sent by One who's True.

And thus, I send this lesson out to you!

*The Spirit of arrogance, pride, condemnation of others, lies, denial

THE HANDS OF GUILT

The hands of guilt cast lurid shadowed shafts,

Of black upon my purity of soul.

Repulsed by self, I drift as on a raft,

Unmoored and lonely, midst cruel, piercing shoals.

My quaking body streams with panic full.

With helplessness I vision Death's dark door.

And weakness draws my will to Satan's* pull,

Distracts me from Christ's steering, guiding oars.

I pray, "Take hold Christ's oars of Love and Hope."

Thus, vanquish condemnation Doubt's cruel friend.

Allow my joy and faith to gather scope,

Augment with Love of Christ, self- treachery end.

It's done! I let Christ help me steer my course.

Dispelled all guilt and fear. Christ's love, The Source.

*The Spirit of arrogance, pride, condemnation of others, lies, denial

TO TRUST ONESELF, A PARADOX

To trust oneself, a paradox of life.

For selves do know a dark and thwarting force,

That overrides sane reason, causes strife,

And hides to avoid exposure of its source.

The trickster spoils contentment with oneself,

Diverts the mind from Spirit's purity,

And tunnels breaches in the heart with stealth,

And makes one see oneself as parody.

But lo! Sweet springs of love do burgeon forth,

And flood the stagnant tarn of dark and death,

With cleansing waters sparkling placid warmth,

To dissipate cruel hatred's fetid breath.

As life and death do grapple, fight for me,

Christ seals my trust and fosters sanctity.

I CALL UPON THE LORD

I call upon the Lord when Doubt is near,

And sins* lay heavy on my wicked heart,

And pain and isolation and the fear

Of self-destruction rend my soul apart.

Christ comes first faintly and my soul uplifts,

As skyward larks take flight from Spring to Spring.

Then strength flows, self-torment Christ sets adrift,

Upon forgiving seas Christ's mercy brings.

How weak my flesh to think I've overcome,

Cruel judgment's scourge that eats into my soul.

Each time I glimpse Beelzebub I run,

Seek Christ to heal, secure me, make me whole.

Without the Lord, I'm Death's toy and its prey.

A corpse, a demon, doubt-filled, self-betrayed.

self-doubt, self-condemnation, doubting God, self-victimization, fear

WHY DO I FEAR?

Why do I fear that which I can't control,

And run from facing Death's dark, cruel land?

Why do I seek those who grasp with tight hold,

My spirit with ungenerous, hateful hand?

Why do I let such forces buffet me,

As wind in fall strikes trees and strips them spare?

Why do I take abuse and cruelty,

As food to swallow in resigned despair?

I look inside and see that which I fear,

Then clasp the outrage to my active self.

I look around at those who'd my life steer,

And sever their rough grasp with mental health.

I face, confront, the force that tears at me.

Unleash my will and shape my destiny.

WHILE STEEPED IN NERVOUS THOUGHTS

While steeped in nervous thoughts a truth came clear.

It pierced my being cold with steel, stark blades,

And pounded revelations that I fear,

That blindness, senselessness I couldn't evade.

The truth proved sound to mine and others' lives,

Could not be daunted by my need to flee.

From out its tentacles that reached full wide,

It circled round to fast encompass me.

I saw my beast-like nature, others' too,

That sought fulfillment of the basest needs;

The kindness, love and selflessness eschewed,

For selfish ends to sate such endless greed.

I saw my sad unworthiness and knew,

That Christ's pure Grace is meant for me and you.

I'VE GONE FROM HOPE AND LIFE

I've gone from hope and life to dark and death,

From dreams that I'd be free to soar and fly,

Create my masterpiece, express my breadth,

In plays' protagonists who live and die.

In hope to thwart life's blows, I would pretend

To be another, passioned and complex,

While running all the while from some cruel end,

I thought I'd fool the fates and fear suppress.

Instead, a grinning evil face emerged,

Which grew in malcontent and lust and blame,

Then married hope with strife to thus deter,

My soul's expression: my growth evolving frame.

Oh, why have I misplaced my love of God?

Let loose the Hounds of Hell* my soul to trod?

Mythological spiritual dog creatures representing torment, savagery, self-brutalization

SUCH DARKNESS AND DEPRESSION

Such darkness and depression fill my soul.

I know nowhere to turn to lift my hopes.

And desolation's weapons take control,

Thus, end my dreams of breadth and light and scope.

Each day I wake to face a fount of fears.

Alone, the darkening clouds devour me.

No one conjoins my mind in peaceful cheer,

For I alone unique see what I see.

I long to be united, strong in love,

Be with an earthly one so safe, so true,

To end the desolation and thus prove,

I'm joined in warmth and safe from sadness too.

But earthly love will never satisfy.

Nor fill my soul like Christ. That dream's a lie.

MOVE

Oh Savior, lift me up. My spirit's low,

And lead me to your pasture soft and warm,

Away from treacherous shoals and labyrinth's woe,

And darkness, smothering will to static forms.

Oh Savior, spur my spirit toward the fields

Of light and rest and peace, sweet action's womb.

Produce momentum; in energy do seal

My essence. Repel the vacuum, inaction's tomb.

Oh Savior, fasten my conscience to your Love.

Fire my will to melt with Yours, then seat,

Me in Your wisdom's throne. And Holy Dove,

Enfold me in Your wings, the void defeat.

Cruel resignation, stasis, and delay,

Are vanquished by Jehovah's Will and Way.

THE PROPHET ISRAEL

The prophet Israel is Christ who's come,

In me, in you. God's light decries all Night.

The ever-present Glory of God's son,

Has conquered sin,* its torment and cruel strife.

No tears of sad, drear sorrow do we shed,

Just tears repentant, joyful, healed by Grace.

So grateful love we feel, for Christ has led

Us to the realm, where we've become Love's face.

Love's hand is ours, Love's eyes are eyes of ours.

Love's breath so sacred breathes throughout our souls.

We stretch our cells, our yearning for Christ's power,

Each molecule of Life to be Christ whole.

Oh Savior, we believe Your Will's the way,

These temples, vessels, worship Christ the Day!

That which separates us from God's love: self-doubt, self-condemnation, self-victimization, fear

A NEW CREATION

Oh Savior! Soar me skyward from Hell's* eyes,

Eyes screaming darkness, stark, cold atmospheres.

Oh, spin and tilt this axis toward sunrise,

Sunrise ebullient, boundless, full of cheer.

Free me from hate-filled eyes that freeze my soul,

Like molten magma hardening to dull rock.

Pluck out Hate's eyes so sightless they extoll,

A different Light in faith, in psychic shock,

That bonded, I'm with them and they're with me,

That Truth transforms and gives them power to change,

That sightless crystal clear in faith they see

Christ's rainbow prisms shine through love proclaimed.

Dear Christ! You let us walk by faith not sight.

Enfolding wisdom, we follow Your infinite Light.

*a spiritual place of doubt, fear, self-condemnation, depression

SAVIOR

My Savior is the One who flames my fire.

My Savior is the Truth that gives me Joy.

My Savior does consume me in desire.

Christ's love and faith in me do fear destroy.

Feel Spirit's presence, though invisible.

So strong It is, It softens me with Grace.

Receiving Spiritual wisdom, my soul is full,

Forever in Peace through Life's cruel hurtling pace.

Christ satisfies my longings and my dreams,

Fulfills that which was void, dark, emptiness.

The Spirit's all to me; it shines, its gleams,

And lightens loads and ends my sad distress.

My Savior is the Lamb, dear Christ, the Lord.

The Light is Truth, in me the Living Word.

THE LORD

The Lord, the Christ, is all that I do see.

No man see I to draw my soul away.

Christ is the One whose Glory shines through me,

Dispels all dark, spreads truth in all pure ways.

Spiritual power and might I do impart,

To those who hunger for sweet righteousness.

Christ's love and joy I share with Godly hearts,

Who do receive my kiss as God's caress.

My hand outstretched is Health to heal sick souls.

My mind like diamonds, Christ's to stately sound,

And break and shatter stasis' death grip hold,

On hearts who'd grow in Christ, once lost, now found.

Infinite riches Christ offers to sinners and saints.

Adjures us in God's love with no constraints.

INCOMPLETE

Without reception of Christ's love and grace,

We live a life that's incomplete, bereft

Of knowing that Christ pleads to God our case,

An advocate who strikes at sin's* soul theft.

We must believe the Spirit's need to fill

Our souls with love, so we can then forgive

Our weakness, foibles, flimsy lack of will,

And prosper in Christ's light and spiritually live.

Without a spiritual walk in faith divine,

Impossible to crucify self-hate,

That leadens will and spins us to decline,

And drains our self-hood to a withering state.

Forever, Christ forgave us, always will.

We must forgive ourselves. Let peace be still.

*self-doubt, self-condemnation, doubting God, self-victimization

THE SOUL OF ALZHEIMER'S

Noted reactions I witnessed with a relative, who had early onset Alzheimer's, encompassed denial, rage and projection. The individual's belief in their own rightness excluded any consideration that there might be other viewpoints. Family members didn't realize what was going on and suffered, believing this individual to be their normal self, as they withstood the suffering individual's wrath.

The process was slow at first, like a frog being dropped into a pot of water whose heat increases until it's too late as the creature is boiled alive. We made excuses as the temperature rose. We normalized the relative's behavior, believing that was the way she always was. The times of fury became more frequent. The criticisms of everyone grew and were picked up and given credence. Judgment and logic fled and incorrect decisions were made based upon the relative's wants and needs. Indeed, the entire world revolved around this individual's psychosis which those around her bowed down to out of love or fear or inability to say, "Something is wrong. What is it?"

Why didn't we recognize the signs? Why did we give her power to condemn and justify her irrational arguments which she believed with her heart and mind because she had to? Her skewed world view was predicated on the hell of her creation spilling out onto "them," "those," "him," "her." And this went on for almost a decade. Finally, bad judgments ended in a car accident and a neck operation that was botched. And the disease was discovered. What she feared all along had come upon her, but it was once again, ignored by her and others. Then, the behavior became so extreme, it could not be ignored. She had to be watched almost 24/7 by family.

By that time the relative moved to Florida and I had become a freelance writer and Entertainment Journalist and my relative seemed to be holding her own but I hadn't visited in a while. My cousin and I went to hear the wonderful David Hyde Pierce speak about his experiences with his grandfather and father having Alzheimer's. He is a spokesperson for the Alzheimer's Foundation and was heartfelt and eloquent.

When I saw him in a play that I reviewed, I stayed after to speak to him and have him sign my program. Though I wasn't planning to, I brought up the subject of Alzheimer's and said that my relative had it. His response astounded me. He looked deeply in my eyes and pierced my soul. He said, "I'm so sorry." It was his sympathy that touched my heart and made me realize that I had been cavalier, ignoring a situation from which I will never recover. My friend/relative was disappearing before my eyes, and there wasn't a damn thing I could do about it.

His empathy for a fellow sufferer allowed me to understand my own blindness, fear and helplessness. Some part of me accepted the realization I had dismissed. I and the family reflected and looked back to the arguments of that time, the fury and diffuse anger at everything. And we understood. All of us had Alzheimer's. All of us were blind and powerless to help.

This was early onset. Currently, there is no cure. It is the sixth leading cause of death in the nation. This sonnet is dedicated to all family who suffer this disease along with their loved ones, who at this time, only may be accurately diagnosed after they have passed.

THE SOUL OF ALZHEIMER'S

Fury braced, the soul cannot take rest.

Bound in bitterness it does retreat,

Within a world of woe and great distress,

And sorrows which the mind cannot defeat.

And like a ship that crashed upon a reef,

Wave battered, smashed, and torn 'til nothing's left,

The mind does lose its sanctity through grief.

Where are health and wholeness? All's bereft!

While doctors search for answers chemical

And soberly discuss the neuron clumps,

The soul's a ghost an empty shell, a hull,

Abyss-lost, disappeared, a black hole dump.

Oh God! Have mercy on this darkened state.

Dear God! Shine love and light upon this fate.

BREAKING THROUGH

When does an individual become his or her own person? Sometimes, never. It may take a village to raise a child, but the child must then strike out on their own and make the world a better place for others. To realize your place in the purpose and scheme of the fabric of life requires constant submission to the divine. It also requires complete trust in what you may not even understand is present or real (God). So the journey is a long one, but there are vibrant illuminating beacons. You are never in the darkness for very long. And when the light is particularly bright, you do see your condition and the state of your life. Then is the moment of decision. Is it possible to be uniquely free to find your passion that is divinely inspired? What do you have to sacrifice to achieve it? Ego? Lies? Bondages? Faith in Christ can be the way toward freedom. And the price has already been paid.

BREAKING THROUGH

The culture shapes and pulls us to its will.

Parents, teachers, pals do tie our souls.

And as we're buffeted by these strange ills,

Ourselves in tangled image we unfold.

We question who we are and what we'd be,

Propelled to think their thoughts. They hold us in.

The lies like walls occlude what we would see.

We're caught. True thought then never does begin.

It takes a lifetime to cut soulish ties,

Be light-filled, free from chains that bind our hands.

It takes great strength to try and try and try,

Promote our independent soul to stand.

And only through Christ's help can we break free,

From cultural folkways to uniquely be.

BLIND

Years ago, I awakened from a nightmare that I remembered. In it, I was driving down the road in complete darkness, a night so black, I couldn't see an inch before me let alone the road. Yet I was driving, somehow moving along and there were others in the car with me. It was in 1987, around the time of the Jessica Hahn, Jim and Tammy Faye Bakker scandal. I made a decision to take a stand against the church she had been a part of and the leadership who supported her. When I woke up, I did and didn't understand the dream, based upon my journey in Christ up to that point. Now, I see its meaning for today and realize it is coming to pass and has come true. I am blind, sighted spiritually.

Upon the road, when driving home at night,
It came to me, a searing, striking flash,
That blind I was. Christ's Love had darkened sight,
And taking up the sword, the Word, I'd slashed,
My trust in physical realms, my senses five.
I'd pierced my physical sight like Oedipus,
And drove the Word to gouge and gore my eyes,
'Til Truth in time became my greatest Trust.
And now Blind Faith embraces all my heart,
Draws me in love toward God who can't be seen.
In me Christ lives. We'll never be apart.
The Spirit fills my days. I know and glean,
The living and the dead, the dark, the light,
The spiritual world, from physical realms of sight. *

*The Word of the Lord counsels us to walk by faith not by sight. This was a long and gradual process for me to understand.

THE DARK WILL NEVER UNDERSTAND THE LIGHT

The Dark* will never understand the light.

The Light allows one's vision to be clear.

The Dark would rob you, stab you through and smite

You with its hate and strife and hellish fear.

The Light is Truth. And once it's come in you,

No living thing can stop its wondrous flow.

For Grace in Christ is Light and Peace and Truth.

The acts of hate the Spirit overthrows.

And I do know the Living Word's in me.

I shout, proclaim the Spirit's experience.

Do know effects of crass idolatries,

Their horrors and their painful recompense.

And now Christ gently shows God ways to me.

The mysteries revealed to make us free.

The Dark: A spiritual entity which encourages blindness and trust in what one can physically see, decrying the realms of Spirit which are not visible to the "naked" eye. (The Light -Christ/Truth requires sight by Faith.)

GOD IN NATURE

‡

LOTUS

The fragrance fragile, hints of frankincense.

The buds so creamy, shaded tapering pinks.

The petals seek the sun in recompense.

From watery darkness muddy roots did drink.

Enfolded in the torpid dank and slime

With faith that soon its glorious day will come,

It waits in dormancy then slowly climbs,

In skyward grace to bask in citrine sun.

How many of your kind just stayed below,

Devoid of spark to seek the spiritual light?

How many not ignited by God's flow

Of love, instead did die in wilted blight?

A miracle each risen Lotus bloom,

A wealth of glorious life born in the gloom.

RED TAILED HAWKS AND MOURNING DOVES

Cacophony of thoughts transport my mind.

I see a red tail spiraling above.

He's waiting on the wind to glean and find

The prey he seeks: the sweet, grey mourning dove.

But Nature, always fickle, lends a hand,

At times protects the sweet and innocent,

Deters the predator from his command,

Displaces and distracts from his intent.

Such comfort do I feel when I observe,

The dove illusive covered by some force

That redirects the red tail in a curve,

And wind-blown sets him off his purposed course.

And I return to peaceful thoughts of Grace

This day the dove escaped and won its race.

CAT HUMAN

I have a feline self that I prefer,

So soft and cuddly, cute and pixie hot,

A feline sharp who loves to trouble stir:

With conservative, political types who're catnip sots.

I gerrymander their powers, possess their souls,

Jump circular crab walks to befuddle them.

Mischievous manipulator, I secure my hold.

With clever paws I pounce, then make amends.

My purring apologies do satisfy.

I cuddle with sweet meows, rub calves and knees,

Seduce them with presumptions I won't decry,

Then wham! Relay the truth of what I see.

For stealth, for truth, for authenticity,

My feline self's, my cloak. It safeguards me.

GALAXIES

The galaxies beyond all hemispheres,

In brilliant song, a chorus of pure rhyme,

Expended elements which did adhere

To vanquish voids, establish space and time.

Exploded stars' magnetic gravity,

Did make solidified the Light of Fire,

Restructured quarks to solar winds and seas,

And set dimensions for galactic empires.

Then sending forth in silent messages

Of consciousness to mirror solid Light,

Transformed all Life in staging vestiges,

Created human beings with power and might.

We're made of stars; astounding truth to see.

I see your face; imagine a galaxy.

SANCTUARY

The New York Botanical Garden reflects God's grandeur in its botanical arrangements and the love, care, mission, and purpose of its caretakers, sponsors, and staff. It is a place of cool asylum where my friends and I hang out, catch up with each other's lives and have dinner at the Hudson Garden Grill. This sonnet celebrates just a bit of what the Garden means to me.

Whenever I am down or feeling blue,

When social, political problems make me lost,

I seek a haven that lifts me unto

A peace that stills my soul if tempest tossed.

The Garden where my friends and I rebound

And laugh and visit the lovely plantings, where

Throughout the seasons there we can be found,

Embracing the floral beauty and exhibits rare.

We visited in grief to uplift our state.

Remember the life of one we did admire.

Anthony Bourdain's cruel death and sorrowful fate,

Resolved with roses and lotus buds inspired.

My hope's always affirmed at NYBG

A spiritual place of vision that sets me free.

ORCHIDACEAE

A fan and journalist covering the New York Botanical Garden exhibits for years, COVID-19 put a crimp in my coverage since the Garden had to close, then adjust to the CDC guidelines for re-opening. However, I am a member. When I can, I visit and add to my digital collection of thousands of photographs of the Garden over the years. A favorite exhibit of mine and all members, sponsors and happy visitors, is the annual Orchid Show. How amazing the themed set up is to feature the Garden's myriad varieties and species of the family Orchidacea. I can't resist purchasing an orchid there. It is my favorite flower along with gardenias which I do not have the right growing conditions for. However, my orchids are happy with me. I must have 30. That is nothing. The head curator of orchids at the NYBG, Marc Hachadourian once had over 100 in his collection. During the pandemic, I wonder if he added to it. Orchids are just an incredible uplift to one's soul.

ORCHIDACEAE

Mysterious family, beauteous, sensual, distinct,

Popularly adored and equally sorrowfully killed,

The purchasers of your stunning gorgeousness think,

You'll live forever in easy care fulfilled.

Research is required to study all your needs.

You crave the humid moisture from the air,

Over watered, nor misted you are aggrieved,

Will wither and rot and die as your owner despairs.

The orchid's a sage, cool judge of human love.

If blooms teased out with patient diligence,

It smiles and basks in secret knowledge of

The owner's love, and botanist's intelligence.

Phalaenopsis, Oncidium, Cattleya too,

God's glorious flowers revered by me and you.

SPARROWS

Sparrows built a nest under a metal overhang in the top corner of my terrace away from the wind and rain. It was a clever construction despite their having to flip upside down to get inside. Last year, the babies and haranguing parents made it difficult for me to bask in the southwest sun during the pandemic, so I decided to remove the nest this year and enjoy my balcony un-pestered. Also, I didn't trust their parenting skills. They were young birds and in previous years they and other birds had babies who died or were near death, struggling and gasping, a tragic sight. I didn't want any more catastrophes, so I took it down. They put it up. I took it down. They continued to build. I took it down and secured electrical tape around the area to thwart their access. My ingenuity worked until mama bird got caught and was hanging upside down swinging at the bottom of the tape.

When I went to release her, she extracted herself and flew away leaving a few tail feathers in the adhesive as a remembrance. I was so devastated, I left them alone to build. But sure enough, initially, they botched the hatchlings. Babies died, and I found six rotting, fly-embraced embryos on the floor of my balcony. Thankfully, they got it right and the singular baby which is still hidden and safe is getting fat on the insects and treats mamma and papa bring her/him continuously. Now, I fear the baby will get so fat, she/he won't be able to wedge out of that space to fly to the trees beyond. I pray I won't have to pick up the pieces if baby crashes and burns on a test run. However, the family have become my pets and when they scold me for watering my plants, I finish quickly and leave them to their important mission of keeping the species alive and wiping out the wayward insect population.

The scriptures are into sparrows for teaching lessons. "Are not two sparrows sold for a penny? Yet not one of them will fall to the ground outside your Father's care." (Matthew 10:29) And if you attended church as I did when I was a little girl, we sang the refrain, "His eye is on the sparrow. I know he watches me." In other words, sparrows are one of the most inconsequential of birds, yet God watches and cares for them. We, as children of God, fashioned after his likeness, are worth more than many sparrows. How much more does God care for us?

Indeed, it is a comforting thought in this time when the Democratic Party and its leadership are concerned for the welfare of U.S. citizens, but the GOP is encouraging us to destroy ourselves with their nihilistic bills (not passed) COVID botch job and attempts to vitiate the constitution and overthrow the democratic processes of our government (Putin welcomed). In that light, citizens are like these slight sparrows. The GOP underestimates them at their own peril. We persist. We build sturdy nests for our children. And God watches the process with a smile on Her face. (July 2021)

Assertively building nests they chirp and sing,

Undaunted if you pull their grass lumps down,

Persist despite your presence. You won't ring

Alarm bells. They're anointed with God's crowns.

Their population burgeoning avians.

Other birds die off, their species wanes.

The mighty sparrow adaptive takes a stand,

Against the climate crisis. They're God sustained.

The craven humans who do despoil Earth's home.

Inflexible and stubborn won't survive.

The kingly sparrow majestic on its throne

Of trees, and bushes and eaves will always thrive.

A lesson we must learn, this creature beloved,

Is fittest in The Grace that's from above.

FIFTY SHADES OF FALL

My home away from home during the pandemic was the New York Botanical Garden. It is a superbly sumptuous garden. It is one of my favorite places in NYC. All the seasons are wild and wonderful there. Fall is the most intriguing because the vegetation is morphing. If you go three weeks in a row, you note the botanical changes which out-herald the leaf-turning of the maples and oaks. Nature's showy Fall production is even more splendiferous and surprising than Spring. The vegetation takes on unusual shapes as it retracts with the colder weather. Every time I've gone there, I notice something unique, and I'm amazed and ashamed to realize I know so little about a landscape so dear to me.

The frost is sculpting grasses, flowers, herbs,

Reforms their structures, so their essence bends.

The wildly fecund scents the air disturbs.

Umber hues to sepia Light transcends.

My senses thrill to apprehend what hovers

In darkening mists, burnt atmosphere so still.

A black squirrel scampers searching for pine cover,

As fading light hydrangea's bowers distills.

Fall ghosts find roses fade, translucent, bronze,

In summer crimson, hot pink, purple, red,

Now iridescent, ashen, grey bygones,

Their citrines shade to mahogany browns, quite dead.

I'm breathless to have visioned this wondrous sight,

Of nature's art, Fall's infinitely hued delights.

THE LAST LOTUS

Crowds of buds have vanished; now yellowed leaves

And dried, brown empty seed pods wind-tossed, bent;

The pond dark, lonely, sorrowfully bereaves

Warm temperatures. Sweet summer's lease is spent.

Fall chafes and nips and bites the unaware,

The rose, hibiscus, and lantanas too,

But this last lotus shivering is aware,

Frost's fiery, brutal nights she can't eschew.

Sink down she must, embrace her watery tomb,

The dark and death hued waters cold and chill.

Inherent in her being is a womb,

That waits for golden days if she stays still.

The human soul, the lotus signifies.

To be reborn eternally in spiritual tides.

AUTHOR'S NOTE

Initially, I was stumped in coming up with a title for this book of sonnets, some of which span over 40 years of writing. Of the few hundred sonnets and poems which have not made it in, some have been lost. The others that I wrote in long hand, I may publish. They are dark and intimately personal. Other sonnets appear on achristianapologistssonnets.com.

In the title I wanted to encompass my relationship to God which began before I was born with Him in "pure light." How do I know I was His? I found some congratulatory cards from members of our church (The First Baptist Church of Patchogue) to my mom on her giving birth to me. One mentioned that the members had been praying that the new baby would know God and would be blessed in her womb even before I was born. I find it ironic now, considering all these years since I read the card, that my father had kept it after my mom died in a car accident with my aunt, a tragedy that our family never fully overcame. It will be 5 decades next year.

Thus, my relationship to God began in my mom's womb and has continued. The ride has been bumpy, difficult and joyful. I have cursed God. I have denied him, embarrassed that I was a believer. I attempted to be an atheist for a time, during college, embracing a kind of oblivion and wantonness born out of my rebellion against the strict, fearful and restrictive attitudes of my parents, who were divided in how much latitude they should give me as a teenager.

When my brother refused to go to church, I followed. My mother still prayed for us. My aunt who was a champion of the spiritual Christ (she had a revelation of his presence when she was baptized) also prayed. I am grateful. Because of their prayers, though I took tremendous risks and skirted the edges of death, I survived and thrived. The danger was that I had spiritual experiences in Christ which opened my eyes to His wonder. But after a relationship which caused heartbreak, I gyrated into the abyss of despair, and angry at Him, negated God.

After one sees Christ's Light, turning one's back on Him is psychic suicide. What made it worse was I embraced the "science" of psychoanalysis for help: a plunge into further darkness. That darkness continued in various shades of dim: a marriage, divorce and additional relationships. Then, I came to the Valley of Decision. I sought God once more and affirmed my faith in Christ.

In the spectrum of light, there are obvious "light shifts." How they occur, and when they occur have been studied at great length, and you can read papers in Physics on light's (wave/particle) movement on a sub-atomic level. I am not a scientist, though the study of matter and light's impact on it has always fascinated me. Spirit and matter, if you will, are at opposites ends of the "spectrum." Do miracles occur in light shifts? Does God embody solid light to create matter? In my imagination, surely. Will science ever "know" Spirit? Surely.

In my life, the movement from light-hope to utter darkness and desolation has gyrated back and forth to widening extremes. These sonnets mirror some of that shifting light. But always undergirding me has been my faith in God, which lifted me up when there was no road, and only the abyss that I had fallen into, the abyss that Christ released me from.

Carole Di Tosti, 2021

OTHER BOOKS BY CAROLE DI TOSTI

PEREGRINE: THE CEREMONY OF POWERS

The supernatural thriller may be ordered on Amazon, Barnes & Noble and on caroleditostibooks.com.

WHISTLEBLOWERS: THE EXPERIENCES OF A SUPERINTENDENT AND TEACHER WHO EXPOSED CORRUPTION IN THEIR SCHOOL SYSTEM

Order number 9411182 UMI 300 N. Zeeb Rd. Ann Arbor, MI 48106

2000+ FILM AND THEATER REVIEWS AND ESSAYS CAN ALSO BE FOUND AT CAROLEDITOSTIBOOKS.COM

www.ingramcontent.com/pod-product-compliance
Lightning Source LLC
Chambersburg PA
CBHW071502080526
44587CB00014B/2183